FRANCES WOODWARD

Phonics Resourc

for Older Learne

Illustrations by Angela Clarke

Phonics Resources for Older Learners

Illustrations by Angela Clarke.

A CIP Catalogue record for this book is available from the British Library

Published by Forward with Phonics 2016
First Published 2012

ISBN 978-0-9935873-0-6

Phonics Resources and Phonics Stories for Older Learners

Printed in Great Britain

Introduction

There is an abundance of phonics resources for use with young children but often the content and tone of the text is unsuitable for an older learner.

I have written this book of resources for teachers of older children and tutors of Adult Literacy and ESOL classes. The phonic progression is that presented in the Sounds~Write programme, but these resources may be useful to any teacher of older learners, who wants to introduce the English alphabet code gradually, in a structured sequence.

For many years I have used the Sounds~Write programme, which is as successful with adult learners as it is with children. Most of the programme can be easily adapted for use with older children and adults. However, the stories have been written with younger learners in mind. A set of stories, suitable for older learners, but which also follow the phonic progression of the programme, can be ordered from www.forwardwithphonics.com .

I have divided this book into two sections.

Section One contains the English Alphabet Code in its simplest form; dealing with the single-letter sounds and consonant digraphs within CVC words at first and gradually increasing the level of difficulty to 5 sound words such as CCCVC. This corresponds to the Initial Code of the Sounds~Write programme and to Phases 2, 3 and 4 of Letters and Sounds.

Section Two deals with the main vowel phonemes in our language and the spellings we use to represent them. This section corresponds to the Extended Code of the Sounds~Write programme and Phases 3 and 5 of Letters and Sounds.

Suitable polysyllabic work is included in each section.

Contents

Section One

Section Two

Resource Book
Section One

Dictation Sentences

There is a set of 12 sentences for each of the following units. They follow the phonic progression that is presented in the Initial Code of the Sounds~Write programme.

The sentences only contain sounds learned up to that point in the programme. The following high frequency words are included: the, is, I, was, for, to, are, all.

These sounds are introduced in a slightly different order in Letters and Sounds and can be found in Phases 2, 3 and 4.

Units 1 and 2 - s, m, t, i, a, n, p, o
Units 3 and 4 - b, c, g, h, d, f, v, e
Units 5 and 6 - k, l, r, u, j, w, z
} in CVC words
Unit 7 - x, y, ff, ll, ss, zz
Unit 8 - VCC, CVCC words, such as 'end', 'lift'
Unit 9 - CCVC words, such as 'stop', 'frog'
Unit 10 - CCVCC, CCCVC, CVCCC words, such as 'drink', 'strap', 'hands'
Unit 11 - <sh>
Unit 11 - <ch>
Unit 11 - <th>
Unit 11 - <ck>
Unit 11 - <wh>, <qu>, <ng>

These sentences can be used in various ways:

1. **As dictation sentences:**
   Read the whole sentence and then repeat slowly, saying one word at a time, while the learners write them down. If there is a high frequency word in the sentence, write it on a whiteboard or card for them to copy.
   Dictate 1-3 sentences in a session, depending on the ability of the learners. It is important for the learners to read the sentences aloud on completion to extend their reading practice and for them to check for meaning.

2. **Sentence Matching:**
   Enlarge the sentences to approximately font size 45-50.
   Print two copies.
   Laminate if desired.
   Cut up all the sentences on both copies.
   Cut up the words on one of the copies. (See over)
   Store individually in small envelopes or cash bags.

The man is on the bus

The	man	is	on	the	bus

Suggested progression for the sentence matching activity.

a) Learners read the sentence then build it with the word cards, as above. They should read the sentence again and write it saying the sounds in the words as they write. When 3-4 sentences are complete, ask them to read them to you.

b) Learners match the words to the sentence, as above. Ask the learner to turn over the sentence card and one of the word cards, before copying the sentence. This challenges them to spell just one of the words on their own and helps to build confidence in spelling.

c) Learners read the sentence. Ask them to turn the sentence over before building it with the separate word cards. Ask them to read the sentence to make sure it is correct before copying it.

d) Learners read the sentence. Ask them to turn it over and write the sentence from memory without the help of the sentence card or separate matching cards. Encourage them to read it again to check it makes sense.

3. **Class Reading Cards:**
Enlarge the sentences to font size 50 - 60.
Laminate and cut into separate sentences.
These can be used as a class reading activity or each learner can be given a different sentence to read and copy.

1. Sit on the mat.
2. It is not Sam.
3. The man is not in.
4. Tom sat on a pin.
5. The map is in the pot.
6. The pin is in the map.
7. The man sat on a mat.
8. The tap is on.
9. The map is on the top.
10. Sip it Tim.
11. It is in the pan.
12. The pot is on the mat.

1. The pan is on the hob.
2. I am in bed.
3. The dog can sit.
4. The man has a mop.
5. Get a fan if it is hot.
6. It is a gas hob.
7. Tom has a big van.
8. The cat is at the vet.
9. Sam has a nap.
10. The man is sad.
11. The cat did not get fed.
12. The pen is in the bag.

1. The man had a bad leg.

2. I ran for the bus.

3. I got to the pub at ten.

4. The dog ran to the man.

5. The jam is in a pot.

6. Ted got his kit bag.

7. Ben met Bob in the pub.

8. The pig is in the mud.

9. Jaz cut his leg.

10. I can sit in the sun.

11. Jim has a pet rat.

12. Rav can win the cup.

1. The van is up the hill.
2. The box is a mess.
3. I will miss the bus.
4. The hot tap is off.
5. Mix it in a pan.
6. The pill is in a box.
7. Jeff will tax his van.
8. Can Bill fix the tap?
9. The fox has six cubs.
10. Jan is not well.
11. The men will get wet.
12. The boss is not in.

1. I will get the jam.
2. The men sit in the pub.
3. Ken got off the bus.
4. Jeff will tell his boss.
5. Is the red pen in the bag?
6. The big box has a lid.
7. It will fill the mug.
8. Maz will fix his van.
9. The kit got wet.
10. The dog ran up the hill.
11. The cat is at the vet.
12. His job is not bad.

1. I will send the gift.
2. Did the belt cost a lot?
3. I can lift the box.
4. The milk is in the jug.
5. Ed went to the bank.
6. The lamp is on the desk.
7. Bill has to mend his tent.
8. The dog will jump in the pond.
9. I must get a hat.
10. The van has a lot of rust.
11. Will I get help?
12. It is in the left hand.

1. The frog can swim in the pond.
2. I plan to stop at ten.
3. Stan went to the golf club.
4. I must not step on the slug.
5. Jen has a pink dress.
6. The crab is on the sand.
7. Brad can spell well.
8. The flag has a red cross on it.
9. The dog can smell a fox.
10. Has the lamp got a plug?
11. The grill pan is hot.
12. Is Jess a twin?

1. I crept up the steps.
2. The tents are all wet.
3. I spent a lot on the dress.
4. The frost melts in the sun.
5. The twins drink from cans.
6. Liz had a big bag of crisps.
7. The dog jumps into the pond.
8. Fred spilt his drink.
9. The van has lots of dents and rust.
10. It melts in his hands.
11. I will stand on the steps.
12. The stamps cost a lot.

1. The shop is shut.

2. Greg has a lot of cash.

3. The brush is in the shed.

4. The cups are on the top shelf.

5. The van was in a crash.

6. I wish I had not got a rash.

7. Shall I get the big dish?

8. I had to rush to the shops.

9. I will get cash from the bank.

10. The fish is in the tank.

11. The crab has a pink shell.

12. Are the shrimps fresh?

1. I can win at chess.

2. Jed sat on the bench.

3. I will chill the drinks.

4. Is the man rich?

5. Chaz had chips for lunch.

6. Shall I chop the logs?

7. It is such a big list.

8. Can I pinch a chunk of flan?

9. The chess set was a gift.

10. Rich got a punch on the chin.

11. I had a chop and chips.

12. I had such a big lunch.

1. I did not think of that.

2. Raf sat with his twin.

3. I got on the sixth bus.

4. I think I was tenth.

5. Beth traps the moth in a mug.

6. This dress is a bit thick.

7. I was the fifth man to jump.

8. I will stand with them.

9. Get a cloth or a mop.

10. That is a thin cloth.

11. I can swim a width.

12. This is his sixth bag of crisps.

1. The duck swims on the pond.

2. I will get a thick jacket.

3. Jack must lock his truck.

4. The man had a shock.

5. The chicks peck at the sack.

6. That is bad luck.

7. The dog ran for the stick.

8. The socks are thick and black.

9. I will lift the pack onto his back.

11. I got a kick on the shin.

12. I must check the lock.

1. I will quit the job.
2. That was a quick quiz.
3. When shall I get lunch?
4. The cat sat on the soft quilt.
5. The ducks quack at the dog.
6. This is a long bit of string.
7. Ring the bell at six.
8. I will bring a tent.
9. Lin sat on the swing.
10. Which song shall I sing?
11. Get the things into the van.
12. Fran sang a sad song.

Picture-Word Matching

There is a sheet containing 10 words and corresponding pictures for each of the following units. They follow the phonic progression that is presented in the Initial Code of the Sounds~Write programme.

The words only contain sounds learned up to that point in the programme.

These sounds are introduced in a slightly different order in Letters and Sounds and can be found in Phases 2, 3 and 4

Units 1 and 2 - s, m, t, i, a, n, p, o
Units 3 and 4 - b, c, g, h, d, f, v, e
Units 5 and 6 - k, l, r, u, j, w, z
Unit 7 - x, y, ff, ll, ss, zz
} in CVC words

Unit 8 - VCC, CVCC words, such as 'end', 'lift'
Unit 9 - CCVC words, such as 'stop', 'frog'
Unit 10 - CCVCC, CCCVC, CVCCC words, such as 'drink', 'strap', 'hands'
Unit 11 - <sh>
Unit 11 - <ch>
Unit 11 - <th>
Unit 11 - <ck>

Ask the learners to read a word from the box and find the picture to match. They then write the word next to the picture, saying the sounds as they write.

This is a useful exercise for ESOL or EAL learners, as it helps to increase their vocabulary.

Hear the learners read the words on completion, as extra reading practice.

Match the words to the pictures:

pot	tap	map	mop	pin
top	sit	pop	man	tin

 ______________

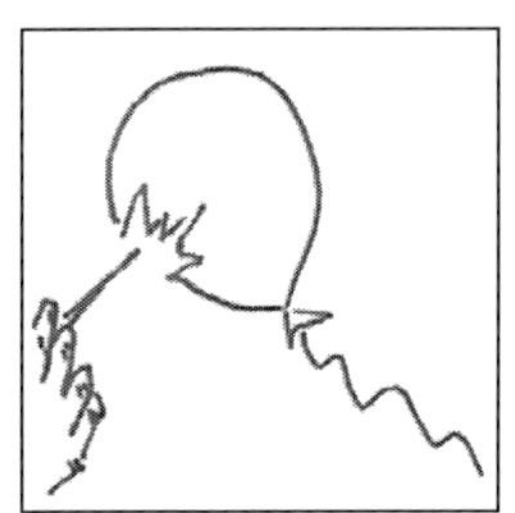 ______________

 ______________

 ______________

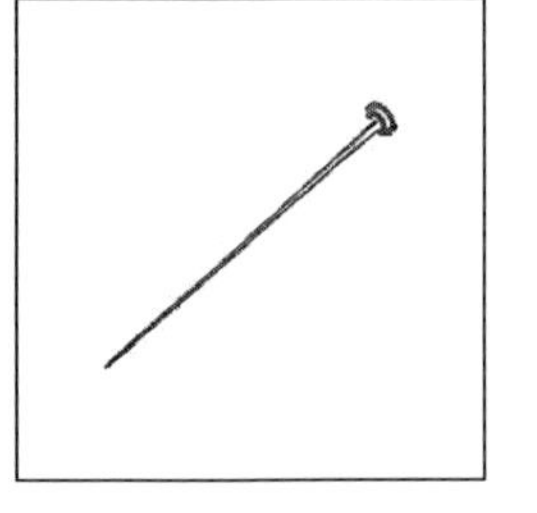 ______________

 ______________

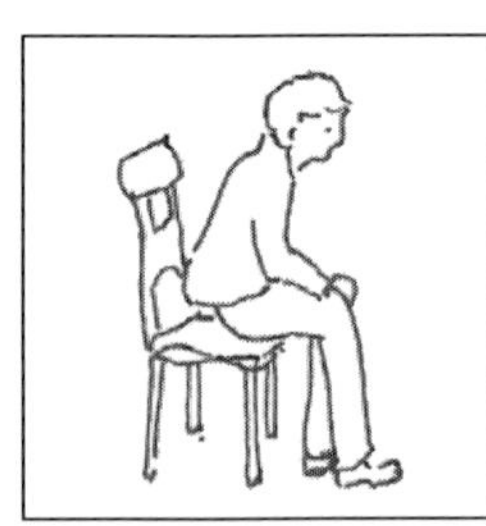 ______________

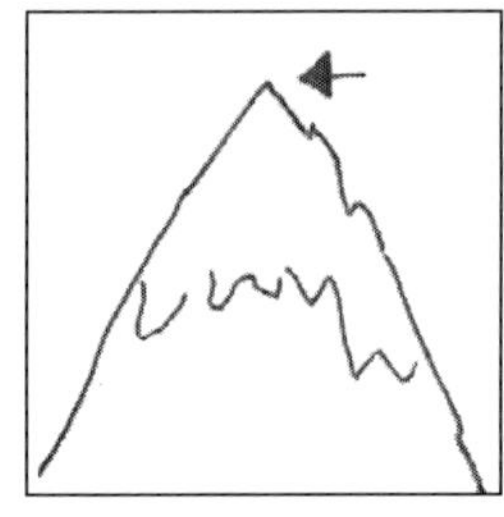 ______________

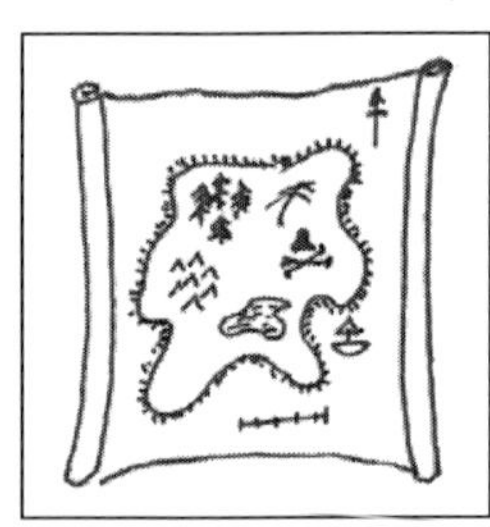 ______________

 ______________

Match the words to the pictures:

bag	hat	van	peg	fan
net	bed	dog	ten	cat

 ____________

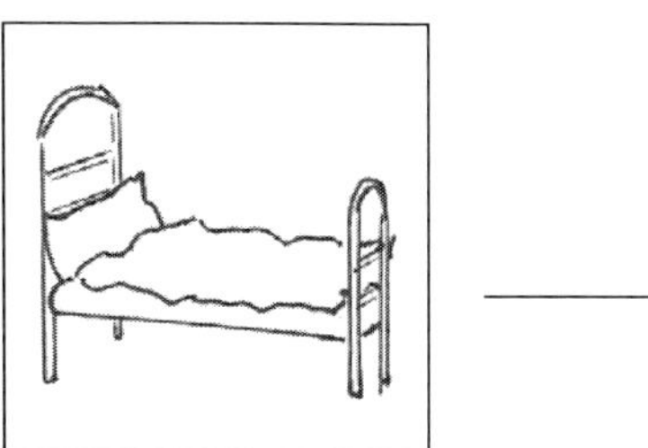 ____________

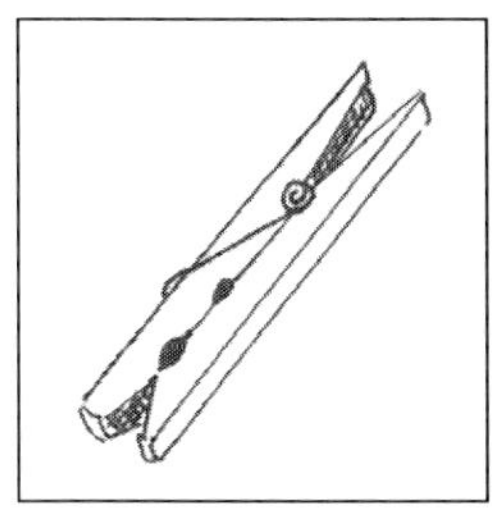 ____________

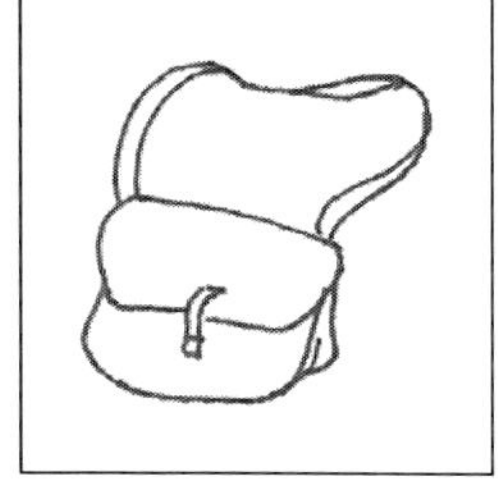 ____________

 ____________

 ____________

 ____________

 ____________

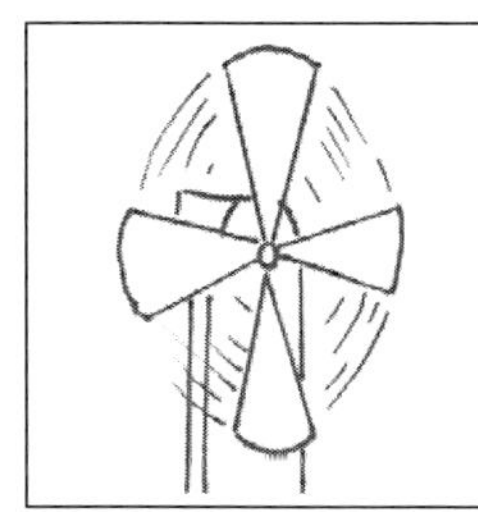 ____________

10 ____________

Match the words to the pictures:

wet	sun	mug	rat	jug
bus	web	zip	leg	jam

Match the words to the pictures:

fox	cuff	mix	yell	box
six	mess	kiss	hill	bell

Match the words to the pictures:

hand	bulb	lamp	vest	milk
desk	pump	belt	tent	wink

Match the words to the pictures:

frog	twin	stop	drum	flag
crab	plug	drill	swim	step

Match the words to the pictures:

skips	steps	stand	plank	drink
scrub	crisps	trunk	strap	hands

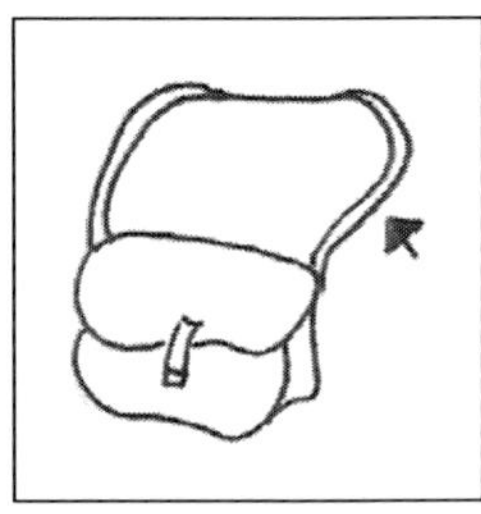

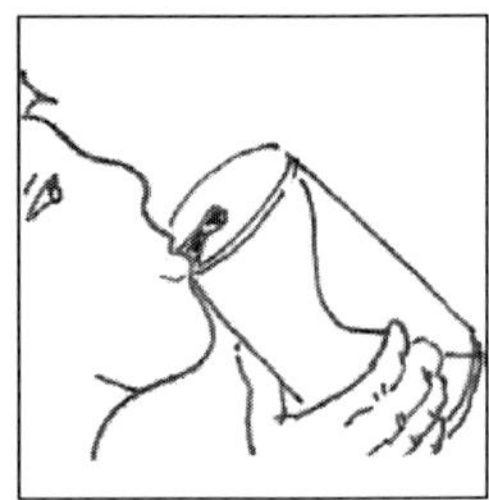

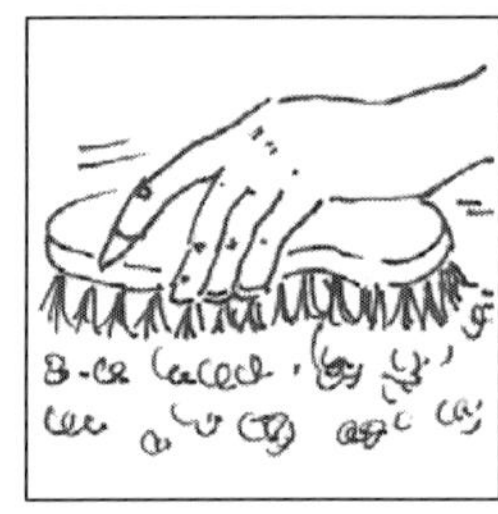

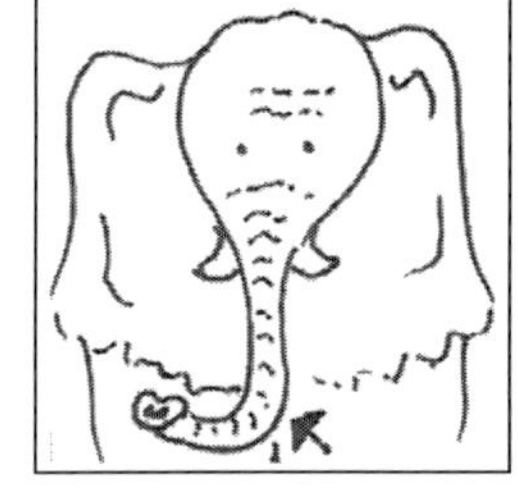

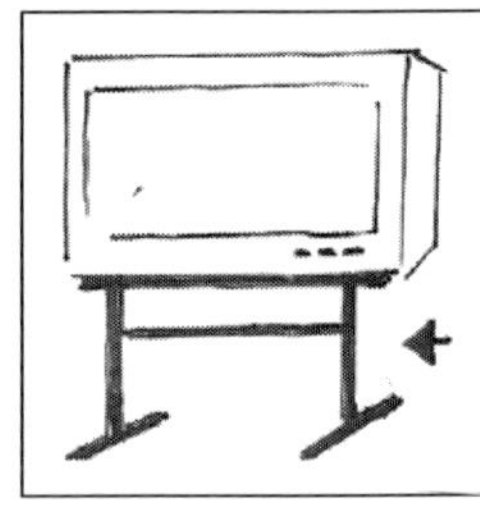

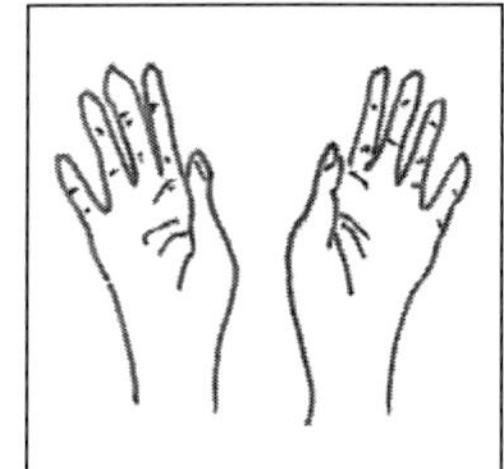

Match the words to the pictures:

shell	dish	shop	cash	brush
crash	ship	fish	shed	shelf

 ______________

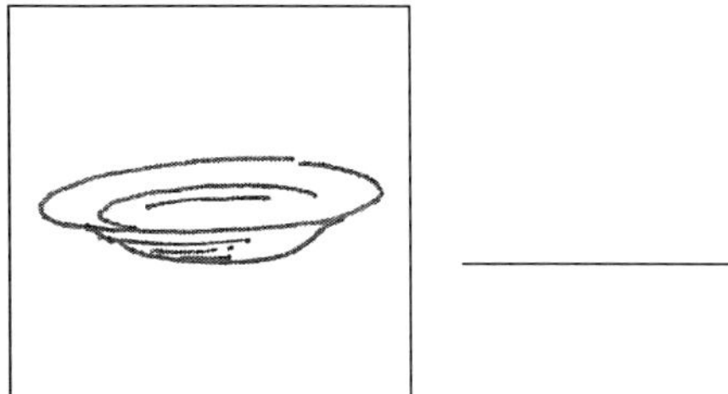 ______________

 ______________

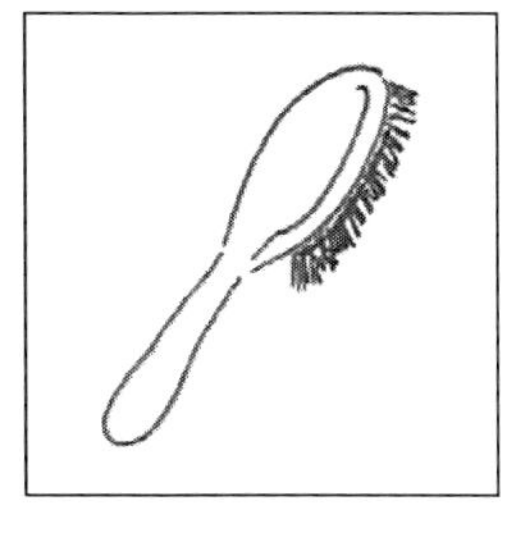 ______________

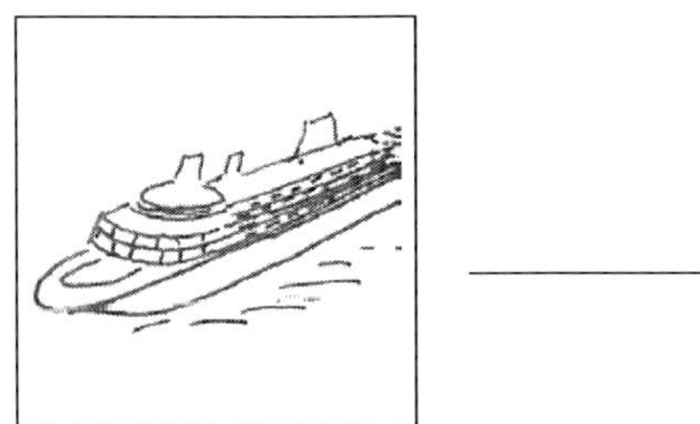 ______________

 ______________

____

 ______________

 ______________

____

Match the words to the pictures:

chips	chess	rich	lunch	chop
bench	punch	chin	chest	bunch

 ____________

 ____________

 ____________

 ____________

 ____________

 ____________

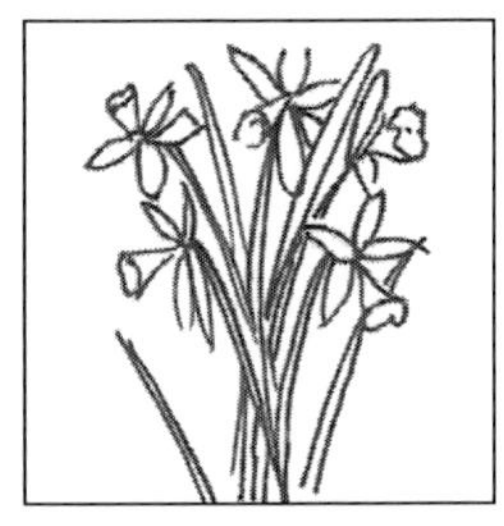 ____________

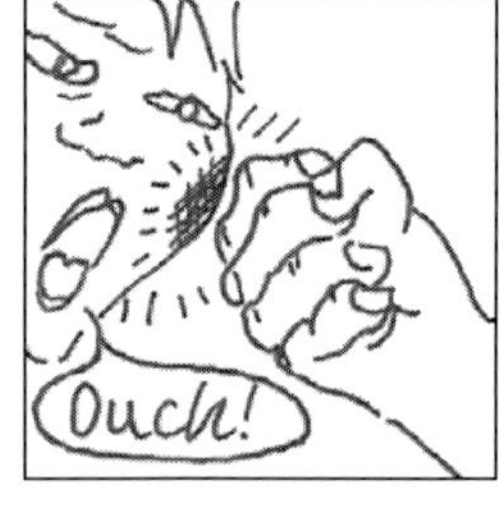

____

____

 ____________

Match the words to the pictures:

thin	cloth	tenth	froth	thick
moth	depth	throb	width	think

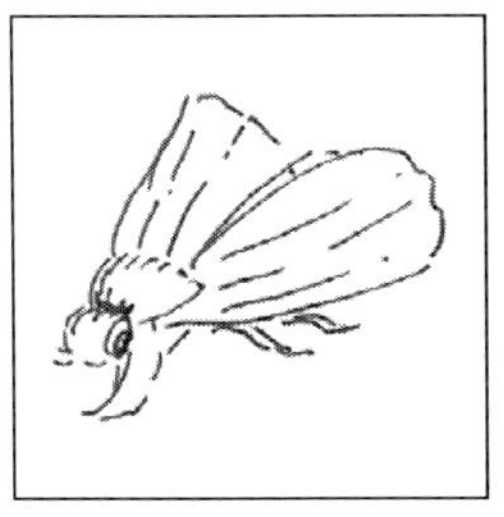

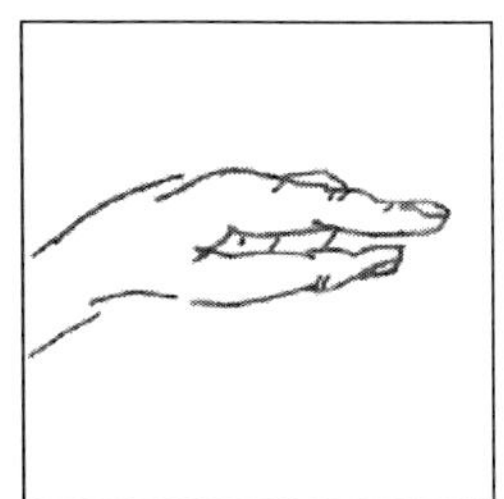

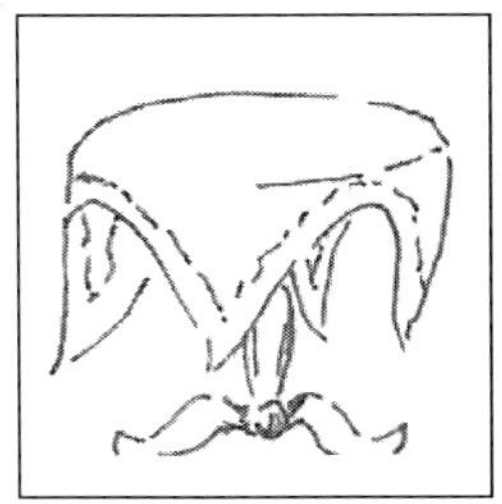

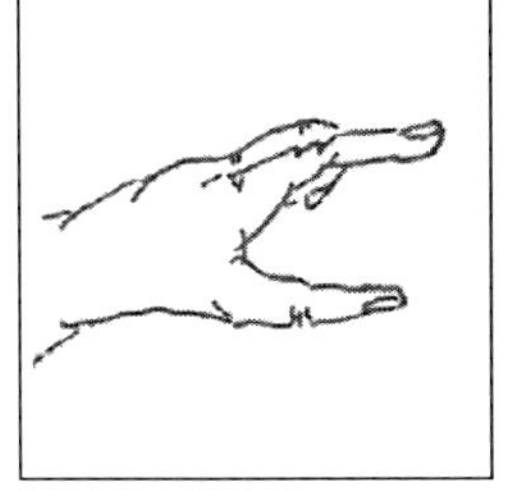

JULY

M	T	W	T	F	S	S
			1	2	3	4
5	6	7	8	9	(10)	11
12	13	14	15	16	17	18
19	20	21	22	23	24	25
26	27	28	29	30	31	

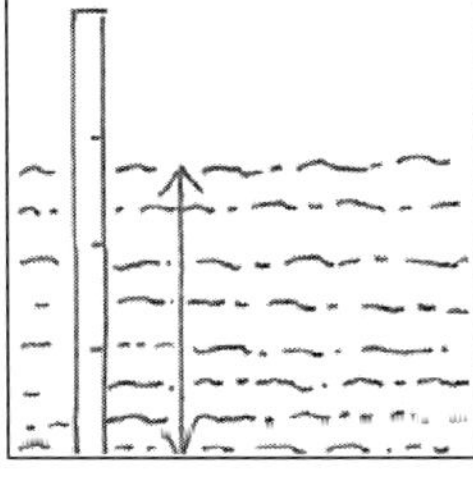

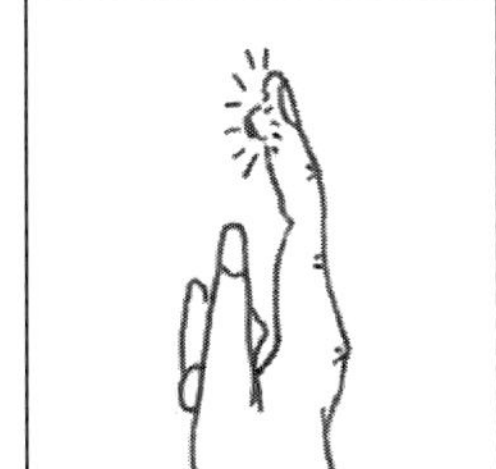

Match the words to the pictures:

back	chick	duck	kick	clock
sack	brick	lick	lock	neck

 ____________

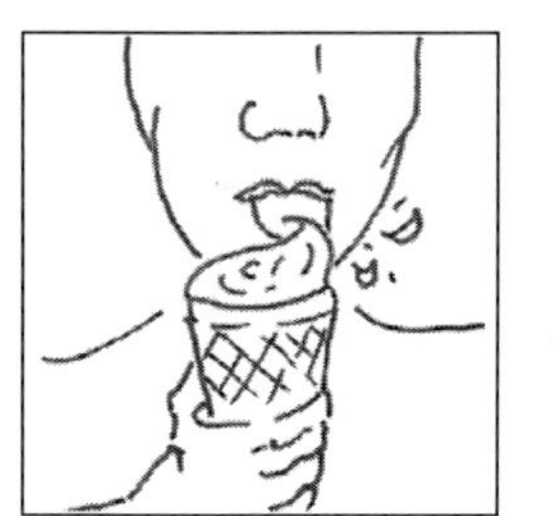 ____________

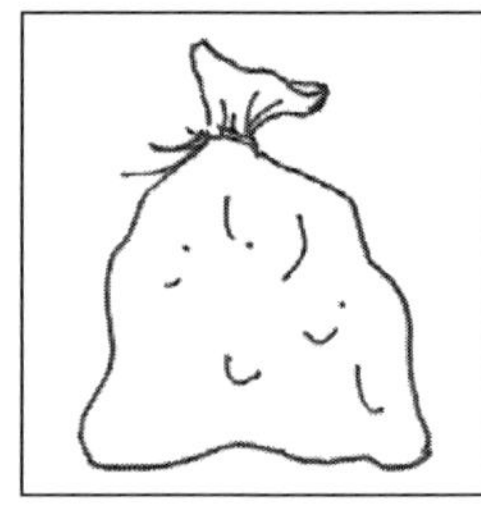 ____________

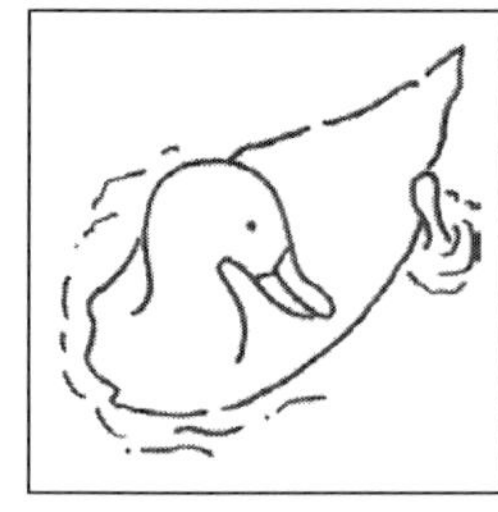 ____________

 ____________

 ____________

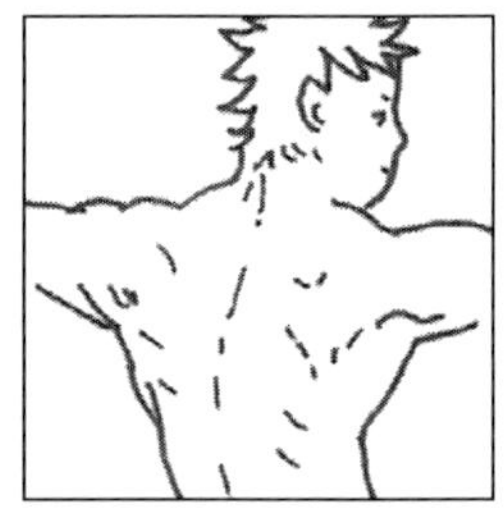 ____________

 ____________

 ____________

 ____________

Match the words to the pictures:

swing	whip	quilt	sing	whisk
quack	hang	king	quiz	quick

Gap-Fills

There is a set of 10 sentences for each of the following units. They follow the phonic progression that is presented in the Initial Code of the Sounds~Write programme.

These sounds are introduced in a slightly different order in Letters and Sounds and can be found in Phases 2, 3 and 4.

Units 1 and 2 - s, m, t, i, a, n, p, o
Units 3 and 4 - b, c, g, h, d, f, v, e
Units 5 and 6 - k, l, r, u, j, w, z
Unit 7 - x, y, ff, ll, ss, zz
} in CVC words

Unit 8 - VCC, CVCC words, such as 'end', 'lift'
Unit 9 - CCVC words, such as 'stop', 'frog'
Unit 10 - CCVCC, CCCVC, CVCCC words, such as 'drink', 'strap', 'hands'
Unit 11 - <sh>
Unit 11 - <ch>
Unit 11 - <th>
Unit 11 - <ck>
Unit 11 - <wh>, <qu>, <ng>

The sentences only contain sounds learned up to that point in the programme. The following high frequency words are included: the, is, I, was, for, to, are, all

In Units 1-10 the learner chooses a word from the box to fill the gap in each sentence.

In Unit 11 the concept of two letters representing one sound is the focus. The sheets for this unit require the learner to add the target digraph to the words in the box. They should be encouraged to say the sounds and the word as they do this. Then they choose words from the box to fit into the sentences.

On completion, hear the learner read the sentences. This enables them to check for meaning and also acts as extra reading practice.

Choose a word from the box for each sentence:

tap	man	pin	mat	sat
pot	top	not	map	tin

1. Sit on the ______.
2. The ______ is on.
3. Tom is a ______.
4. Pam is ______ a man.
5. The ______ is in the tin.
6. Tim ______ on the mat.
7. Pop the pip in a ______.
8. The ______ is on the tin.
9. Is it in the ______.
10. The ______ is on the top.

Choose a word from the box for each sentence:

bad	dog	fed	van	hot
pen	fan	bed	gas	vet

1. The ______ is his pet.
2. Meg ______ the cat.
3. The pan is on the ______.
4. Tim has a ______ in his bag.
5. Get the ______ if it is hot.
6. Dan is a ______.
7. The man had a ______ hip.
8. Sam is in ______.
9. Tom has a big ______.
10. The hob is ______.

Choose a word from the box for each sentence:

man	bus	job	gun	rat
jam	cat	cut	red	wet

1. I got on the _____.

2. The _____ sat on his lap.

3. Kim got the _____.

4. The _____ pot has a lid.

5. The man had a _____.

6. Ken _____ his leg.

7. Get the _____ mug.

8. Ted had a pet _____.

9. The dog bit the _____.

10. Jan got _____.

Choose a word from the box for each sentence:

van	bill	mess	fox	fell
jog	miss	boss	hill	box

1. The man ran up the ______.
2. The ______ has a lid.
3. Jill ______ in the mud.
4. Rex will sell his ______.
5. The ______ has six cubs.
6. The hut is in a ______.
7. Max had a ______ up the hill.
8. I will ______ the bus.
9. Jeff is the ______.
10. I will get the ______.

Choose a word from the box for each sentence:

milk	help	bulb	gift	cost
film	gets	mend	sits	loft

1. The _____ is in a box.
2. The belt _____ a lot.
3. The _____ is sad.
4. Mel _____ the cups.
5. Is the box in the _____?
6. The _____ is in the lamp.
7. Bill will _____ the tap.
8. Can I _____?
9. Jess _____ on the sand.
10. The _____ is in the jug.

Choose a word from the box for each sentence:

drop	plug	stop	cross	dress
crab	drill	trap	frog	smell

1 The ______ is red.

2. Brad got the ______ from his van.

3. The ______ digs in the sand.

4. Has the lamp got a ______?

5. I can ______ the jam.

6. The rat is in the ______.

7. I must not ______ the cups.

8. The ______ can swim in the pond.

9. Fred can ______ the drip.

10. The flag has a red ______ on it.

Choose a word from the box for each sentence:

swept	dusts	belts	stand	mends
drops	spilt	clips	crisps	frost

1. I had to ________ on the bus.
2. Fred ________ the big box.
3. I had a bag of ________.
4. Greg ________ up the mess.
5. Fran has six ________.
6. The sun melts the ________.
7. Bev ________ the desk.
8. I ________ the milk.
9. The pen ________ on to the pad.
10. Frank ________ the lamp.

Add 'sh' and read the words:

_op	wi_	_ut	cra_	ca_
di_	_ed	fi_	bru_	_rink

Choose a word from the box for each sentence:

1. The ______ swim in the pond.
2. The ______ is shut on Sunday.
3. I ______ him lots of luck.
4. Scott had a ______ in his van.
5. I will ______ up the mess.
6. I can get ______ from the bank.
7. The ______ is in the sink.
8. I get the drill from the ______.
9. The shops ______ at six o'clock.
10. The dress will ______ if it gets wet.

Add 'ch' and read the words:

__op	ri__	__ill	lun__	mun__
su__	pun__	__at	__ips	__ess

Choose a word from the box for each sentence:

1. I will ______ the logs.
2. The rabbit will ______ the carrots.
3. The ______ man has lots of cash.
4. Josh got a ______ on the chin.
5. It is ______ a sad film.
6. Can I have ______ with the fish?
7. Mrs Chan and Mrs Trim have a long ______.
8. I had chicken and chips for ______.
9. I bet I can win at ______.
10. I will ______ the drinks.

Add 'th' and read the words:

__em	mo__	__at	fif__	clo__
ten__	__ick	__is	__ink	__ank

Choose a word from the box for each sentence:

1. The ______ is wet.
2. This is a ______ jacket.
3. I must ______ Ben for the gift.
4. I am the ______ man to get on this bus.
5. The ______ is big and black.
6. ______ was a big bag of chips.
7. I ______ I must get fit.
8. Sam is ______ and Brad is sixth.
9. I will get ______ to send the drum kit.
10. I must get help to lift ______ box.

Add 'ck' and read the words:

chi__	cra__	lu__	du__	ki__
thi__	clo__	ba__	pa__	de__

Choose a word from the box for each sentence:

1. I wish Jack the best of ______.
2. Can I sit on the ______ of the ship?
3. The hen had a ______.
4. The ______ struck ten.
5. The ______ swims on the pond.
6. I will ______ my bag.
7. The man has a bad ______.
8. Mick gets a ______ on the shin.
9. It is hot in this ______ jacket.
10. The jug had a ______ in it.

Underline the spellings 'wh', 'ng' or 'qu' and read these words:

wing	which	quiz	lungs	bring
quick	swing	whisk	when	quilt

Choose a word from the box for each sentence:

1. Fran fell from the ______.
2. This is a thick ______.
3. I shall ______ the cups.
4. Jack will ______ the milk and eggs.
5. The ______ was in the pub.
6. The robin has a bad ______.
7. The ______ fox ran from the man with a gun.
8. I will get lunch ______ I get back.
9. The ribs protect the ______.
10. ______ shelf is it on?

Mixed-up Sentences

This is an exercise to help with sentence structure and making a sentence make sense. The learner is given a mixed up sentence and has to sort out the correct word order and write it on the line underneath.

The learners can be told to look out for the word starting with a capital letter, as that will indicate that word should be at the beginning of the sentence.

For extra reading practice, ask the learners to read each sentence while you check them.

There is a set of 10 sentences for each of the following units. They follow the phonic progression that is presented in the Initial Code of the Sounds~Write programme.

The sentences only contain sounds learned up to that point in the programme. The following high frequency words are included: the, is, I, was, for, to, are, all

These sounds are introduced in a slightly different order in Letters and Sounds and can be found in Phases 2, 3 and 4.

Units 1 and 2 - s, m, t, i, a, n, p, o
Units 3 and 4 - b, c, g, h, d, f, v, e
Units 5 and 6 - k, l, r, u, j, w, z
Unit 7 - x, y, ff, ll, ss, zz
} in CVC words

Unit 8 - VCC, CVCC words, such as 'end', 'lift'
Unit 9 - CCVC words, such as 'stop', 'frog'
Unit 10 - CCVCC, CCCVC, CVCCC words, such as 'drink', 'strap', 'hands'
Unit 11 - <sh>
Unit 11 - <ch>
Unit 11 - <th>
Unit 11 - <ck>
Unit 11 - <wh>, <qu>, <ng>

Put these into sentences:

1. on mat. Sit a

2. not man in. The is

3. tap The is on.

4. It pan. is the in

5. in pit. Tip the it

6. the is map. The in pin

7. pot on The top. the is

8. it Sip Tim.

9. the pit. Tom in is

10. not the on top. The is map

Put these into sentences:

1. in bag. the pen The is

2. dad. Ted a is

3. cat. the Bev fed

4. a Dan vet. is

5. bed. on cat The is the

6. Sam pen. the hid

7. the is The pan on hob.

8. the bit man. dog The

9. hat? it a Is big

10. fit. get can I

Put these into sentences:

1. zip can the up bag. I

___

2. jam the in is pot. The

___

3. bus. I get can the

___

4. sit Jan the and sun. Kim in

___

5. has red a Jim kit.

___

6. is The rug wet.

___

7. in dog the mud. dug The

___

8. job Ken a in got pub. the

___

9. cut The his man leg.

___

10. rat run. A can

___

Put these into sentences:

1. will the up hill. run I

2. win Jeff the will cup.

3. got bus. Ken off the

4. rid mess. I get the will of

5. six will mugs. fill I

6. not yet. is It hot

7. the fix tap. can Bill

8. will bus. miss Jeff the

9. on lid box. the is The

10. sell van. Rex will his

Put these into sentences:

1. in Sam bed. is

____

2. in cap the His mud. fell

____

3. ran man. The up the to dog

____

4. the fix I tap. will

____

5. has cub. The a fox

____

6. pills box. The in are a

____

7. hat. a red Meg has

____

8. the cat. Dan fed

____

9. tax van. the will I

____

10. hill. Jim up will jog the

____

Put these into sentences:

1. bank. went I the to

2. wet. sand is The

3. is red. vest His

4. loft. The in box the is

5. on lamp The desk. is the

6. camp. is Tom at

7. box. I lift the can

8. gift. a pen The is

9. cost Did van the lot? a

10. hill. went the I up

Put these into sentences:

1. went Dan golf to club. the

____

2. plug sink. in The is the

____

3. drip. has The a tap

____

4. pond. The in is frog the

____

5. hot? Is the grill

____

6. fell I the on step.

____

7. it the Drop in bin.

____

8. sat cliff. the I on

____

9. twin. a is Fred

____

10. rat trap. The in the is

____

Put these into sentences:

1. till Brad ten. slept

2. the stops The on hill. van

3. swept mess. Ben up the

4. is hot. The drink

5. six Shall get I stamps?

6. up steps. crept the Glen

7. spent Tess on lamp. the lot a

8. the trust twins. can I

9. and crisps drink. Frank had a

10. frost The melt. will

Put these into sentences:

1. brush will dog. I the

___

2. shut. The is shop

___

3. the shelf. on The is jug

___

4. from I bank. cash get the

___

5. a the crash? van in Was

___

6. fish tank. in The is a

___

7. to I the shops. went

___

8. shell The was on sand. the

___

9. bus. rush I to must the get

___

10. wish fit. I was I

___

Put these into sentences:

1. is rich. man The

2. lunch. for I chips had

3. the chop logs. man The will

4. big a such van. is It

5. the chin. on Ken hit got

6. bench? I sit the Can on

7. chat. a rings Fran for

8. a big was punch. That

9. was sad It film. such a

10. I pinch Can a crisp?

Put these into sentences:

1. is cloth wet. The

2. his trip. fifth is This

3. went him. with I

4. this big. I is a think bit

5. swim width? Can a Dan

6. top. Beth thin a has

7. a cost drink That lot.

8. thank man. the will I

9. moth lamp. The on is the

10. trusts Kim them.

Put these into sentences:

1. bad man The a has back.

2. gets truck. in Mick his

3. The the shed. in sack is

4. bags. must I the pack

5. shock? a big it Was

6. the Lock shed. up

7. sat the eggs. duck The on

8. stick. ran the for dog The

9. ten. struck clock The

10. locks. will the I check

Put these into sentences:

1. a of long string. is That bit

2. the When quiz? is

3. I Which sing? will song

4. hand. got the stung I on

5. and thick quilt The soft. is

6. six. at bells The ring

7. clings his Sam Mum. to

8. bag. will I bring the

9. cat. the quacks The duck at

10. eggs. whisk will I the

Wordsearches

This is a useful exercise to be given at the end of a class or as homework. Its purpose is to give extra reading practice, as well as being fun. However, be aware that wordsearches can be completed without it being necessary to read the words! It is important, therefore, for the learner to read the word and then say the sounds as they draw a circle round the word in the wordsearch. Hear the learner read the words to you on completion of the task.

There is a wordsearch for each of the following units. These follow the phonic progression that is presented in the Initial Code of the Sounds~Write programme. These sounds are introduced in a slightly different order in Letters and Sounds and can be found in Phases 2, 3 and 4.

Units 1 and 2 - s, m, t, i, a, n, p, o
Units 3 and 4 - b, c, g, h, d, f, v, e
Units 5 and 6 - k, l, r, u, j, w, z
Unit 7 - x, y, ff, ll, ss, zz
} in CVC words

Unit 8 - VCC, CVCC words, such as 'end', 'lift'

Unit 9 - CCVC words, such as 'stop', 'frog'

Unit 10 - CCVCC, CCCVC, CVCCC words, such as 'drink', 'strap', 'hands'

Unit 11 - <sh>

Unit 11 - <ch>

Unit 11 - <th>

Unit 11 - <ck>

Unit 11 - <wh>, <qu>, <ng>

i	m	a	t	n	b	t	e	m	t
o	n	d	m	h	a	a	t	c	o
s	b	w	u	t	l	s	i	m	p
f	s	i	h	p	a	t	r	d	e
p	a	n	d	t	b	c	t	l	s
f	b	m	s	i	j	s	a	e	i
e	n	d	a	r	g	o	p	h	t
h	p	o	t	w	d	m	a	n	k
b	w	e	s	i	h	i	d	l	e
s	d	m	o	s	m	o	p	n	r

Find these words:

pat sit

top pan

is mat

tap pot

mop man

w	i	c	a	t	s	e	y	l	u
d	r	h	k	x	f	i	t	u	y
h	a	t	c	a	e	h	m	n	h
t	s	p	e	c	a	p	l	o	o
d	b	i	d	g	i	p	a	d	t
o	h	n	i	c	n	u	k	j	y
g	i	x	t	d	v	i	v	e	t
c	v	w	h	e	k	b	l	d	i
m	a	s	f	b	i	g	y	b	u
a	n	c	g	t	u	z	r	p	o

Find these words:

dog	fit
hat	big
vet	van
hot	cap
cat	pin

x	r	d	i	f	h	w	i	n	z
s	e	b	m	o	l	g	b	u	c
w	y	u	k	t	j	a	m	v	d
g	e	t	f	b	i	j	b	w	i
h	m	k	l	e	z	h	u	d	k
m	u	g	r	e	i	x	n	m	i
d	w	o	f	b	p	k	u	h	t
l	a	u	p	j	t	s	w	e	t
e	c	w	l	u	r	v	n	i	e
g	x	a	z	b	r	a	t	d	j

Find these words:

kit wet

mug zip

up win

but rat

leg jam

k	u	b	o	x	s	w	v	x	m
n	y	e	m	o	t	r	d	c	i
m	k	l	p	f	e	g	t	a	x
i	h	l	z	w	y	n	k	f	a
s	v	j	a	h	p	i	l	l	p
s	u	m	o	c	s	j	w	x	v
b	i	l	f	s	t	u	k	g	b
c	u	f	f	n	r	e	z	i	o
m	g	e	t	d	a	s	y	e	s
h	u	r	l	f	b	c	m	z	s

Find these words:

mix	pill
box	bell
yes	miss
tax	boss
off	cuff

w	f	m	i	l	k	i	j	m	p
d	a	g	h	r	j	n	u	i	d
c	r	e	y	d	k	t	x	n	o
s	u	h	u	m	t	e	n	t	g
w	s	k	v	s	l	y	i	d	j
x	t	n	b	e	n	d	t	k	l
i	g	e	w	c	r	a	h	p	a
h	a	n	d	d	t	m	j	i	m
d	v	e	h	o	n	p	u	m	p
r	b	g	o	l	f	s	o	l	b

Find these words:

hand	mint
tent	lamp
milk	rust
bend	golf
damp	pump

z	f	i	k	f	e	g	j	m	l
c	l	u	b	w	d	s	p	o	t
s	a	h	n	r	o	c	b	v	r
a	g	t	k	d	r	u	m	p	i
y	b	p	m	o	u	f	y	i	p
s	w	l	g	j	s	t	o	p	k
d	y	u	n	v	w	x	q	j	i
t	r	g	u	h	i	b	s	u	m
s	d	o	w	z	m	v	n	i	l
t	w	i	n	y	d	g	r	a	b

Find these words:

spot trip

grab stop

club twin

drum flag

swim plug

f	d	y	e	s	j	a	k	o	l
c	r	i	s	p	s	v	x	m	u
w	i	g	t	l	h	u	n	l	t
d	n	r	b	i	m	i	t	w	r
c	k	h	s	t	a	n	d	n	u
t	y	z	t	g	o	t	r	e	s
w	l	y	r	j	f	r	o	s	t
i	n	d	a	t	w	a	p	i	r
n	x	v	p	m	u	e	s	j	l
s	d	t	z	h	p	r	i	n	t

Find these words:

frost strap

twins trust

print drink

crisps stand

split drops

d	r	u	s	h	i	p	v	t	a
c	a	s	h	g	n	e	m	w	s
o	k	r	u	w	c	r	a	s	h
m	d	o	t	p	f	b	s	h	o
z	t	k	p	e	w	m	h	v	P
s	h	r	i	n	k	l	t	x	y
h	e	u	r	q	c	g	j	b	f
i	z	s	h	e	l	f	v	k	i
f	w	h	k	i	d	m	y	g	s
t	j	u	s	x	b	r	u	s	h

Find these words:

fish	rush
shrink	shelf
crash	shop
shut	shift
cash	ship
brush	mash

g	b	e	n	c	h	j	i	l	c
a	w	f	b	h	m	y	r	k	h
e	c	t	h	e	l	o	c	g	i
c	h	e	s	s	n	c	h	o	P
z	a	v	r	t	g	k	i	m	s
w	t	g	p	u	b	c	l	o	k
s	f	x	i	b	y	e	l	h	r
a	b	u	n	c	h	i	r	n	i
d	t	b	c	j	o	r	l	m	c
s	u	c	h	d	l	u	n	c	h

Find these words:

such chop
chat rich
lunch chill
chess chest
bunch pinch
chips bench

r	t	h	a	n	k	u	b	s	t
d	h	q	j	p	m	v	e	k	h
c	e	l	n	y	o	t	l	r	i
l	m	o	t	h	y	h	j	b	s
o	e	x	a	u	k	i	p	n	c
t	w	g	t	h	i	n	b	t	e
h	w	z	h	e	g	k	y	h	l
a	i	b	i	y	m	e	d	e	j
s	t	e	n	t	h	j	n	f	i
v	h	y	g	f	t	h	a	t	c

Find these words:

this	moth
thank	theft
cloth	tenth
that	them
thing	think
with	thin

s	g	u	e	x	b	r	i	c	k
t	j	v	c	m	a	s	o	b	i
i	c	f	h	j	c	l	p	v	c
c	y	n	e	c	k	w	g	h	k
k	i	x	c	b	n	d	e	p	z
w	g	u	k	a	l	u	c	k	t
s	d	h	l	f	w	c	z	j	s
i	t	e	w	z	n	k	m	e	o
c	l	o	c	k	y	o	d	r	c
k	p	j	x	e	g	l	i	c	k

Find these words:

neck	back
lick	kick
sock	duck
sick	clock
luck	stick
brick	check

w	h	i	c	h	f	w	h	e	n
d	a	v	n	a	k	h	i	l	h
s	r	k	u	n	b	i	m	v	z
t	h	i	n	g	o	s	i	n	g
a	x	n	e	t	n	k	y	f	c
w	z	g	d	y	b	n	l	i	d
h	e	j	t	k	r	v	h	o	q
e	b	r	q	u	i	c	k	m	u
r	a	x	h	y	n	j	n	r	i
e	w	l	o	n	g	z	v	l	t

Find these words:

quit	long
king	sing
when	hang
thing	quick
which	whisk
bring	where

Two Syllable Words

This section is in three parts: Word Lists, Word Cards and Worksheets.

Word Lists

It is possible to teach polysyllabic words while working in Section One. This is equivalent to the Initial Code of the Sounds-Write programme and to Phases 2, 3 and 4 of Letters and Sounds. As soon as the learners have gained perfect or near perfect blending and segmenting skills, start with two syllable compound words, then move onto any two syllable words which contain only the sounds taught in this section.

There are two lists in this section:

1. Compound Words
2. Other two syllable words containing only the sounds taught in this section.

Word Cards

There are two pages of two syllable words which can be printed, laminated and cut up to use as word cards for word reading and writing.

These cards can also be used as word puzzles.

1. Print, laminate and cut the word list into separate words.
2. Cut each word into 2 syllables, as a puzzle. Make each one a different pattern, as illustrated below.
3. Put into packs of 8-10 words in small envelopes or cash bags.

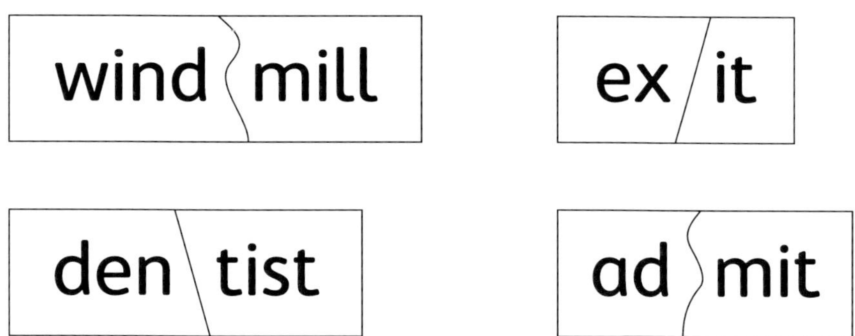

Using the Word Puzzles

1. Learners find all the first syllables by looking for the straight edge on the left, then say the first syllable. They complete each puzzle by finding the second syllable. Learners should say the syllables then the whole word.
2. When all the words are complete, the learners can write the words saying the sounds and the syllables, then the word.
3. More competent learners could then put each word into a sentence.

Worksheets

There are two pages for practising writing two syllable words and two pages of gap-fill exercises using two syllable words, containing only the sounds introduced in this section.

2 Syllable – Compound Words

backchat
backdrop
backhand
backlog
backrest
backstop
backup
bandit
bandstand
batman
bedbug
blackjack
cabin
candid
catnap

checkup
chestnut
chinstrap
chopsticks
desktop
dipstick
dogleg
dustbin
eggshell
flagship
flatfish
frogman
gunman
hamstring
handbag

handclap
helpless
kidnap
lipstick
lunchbox
padlock
pinprick
sandbag
sandbank
sandpit
upset
windmill
within

2 Syllable Word List

(be aware that some words contain a schwa)

acting
admit
adult
assist
atlas
atom
attach
attack
attempt
attend
attract
axis
backchat
backing
bandit
banish
bankrupt
bishop
blinking
Bovril
Brazil
British
cabin
cactus
cadet
candid
cannon
cannot
canvas
checkup
cherub
chestnut
chicken
children
chilli
chopping
chopsticks
collect
comet
comic
comma
comment
complex
conga
connect
consent
contact
contest
contract
convex
convict
correct
cosmic
costing
cotton
credit
cricket
crisscross
crumpet
dandruff
dashing
desktop
dentist
discuss
dismiss
distant
distress
dollop
dustbin

dusting
edit
eggshell
ending
exempt
exist
exit
expel
extinct
fabric
finish
Finland
fishing
frogman
gallop
gunman
handbag
hamstring
happen
helmet
helpless
insult
invent
jackpot
kidnap

kingdom
lunchbox
magnet
mammoth
mattress
mimic
nonstop
nutmeg
object
obstruct
ostrich
padlock
parrot
pocket
polish
pregnant
present
profit
project
public
publish
punish
puppet
rabbit
radish

ribbon
rocket
rubbish
sandpit
second
select
shopping
sluggish
spelling
splendid
stocking
subject
sudden
suspect
triplet
trumpet
undress
until
upset
vanish
visit
wigwam
windmill
wisdom
within

admit	adult
attach	bankrupt
British	cabin
collect	comic
complex	confess
contact	contest
convict	correct
credit	dentist
discuss	distress
dustbin	edit
eggshell	exist
exit	extinct
fabric	fishing

handbag	illness
insult	jackpot
kidnap	object
obstruct	padlock
polish	profit
public	publish
punish	rabbit
rubbish	sandpit
shopping	splendid
subject	suspect
undress	until
upset	vanish
visit	windmill

Two Syllable Words

Read the word. Write one syllable on each line and then the whole word underneath:

hand-bag ____ ____
____

rabb-it ____ ____
____

dust-bin ____ ____
____

tenn-is ____ ____
____

ex-it ____ ____
____

egg-shell ____ ____
____

sub-ject ____ ____
____

pub-lic ____ ____
____

rubb-ish ____ ____
____

pock-et ____ ____
____

shopp-ing ____ ____
____

den-tist ____ ____
____

pas-ta ____ ____
____

in-vent ____ ____
____

a-dult ____ ____
____

hus-band ____ ____
____

a-ddress ____ ____
____

chil-dren ____ ____
____

Two Syllable Words

Read the word. Write one syllable on each line and then the whole word underneath:

pun-ish	____ ____ ________	up-set	____ ____ ________
vic-tim	____ ____ ________	vis-it	____ ____ ________
sand-wich	____ ____ ________	con-tact	____ ____ ________
pol-ish	____ ____ ________	spell-ing	____ ____ ________
in-sect	____ ____ ________	Brit-ish	____ ____ ________
ill-ness	____ ____ ________	wedd-ing	____ ____ ________
fin-ish	____ ____ ________	fab-ric	____ ____ ________
pock-et	____ ____ ________	pad-lock	____ ____ ________
ad-mit	____ ____ ________	un-til	____ ____ ________

Choose a word from the box for each sentence:

upset	dentist	polish	shopping	sandwich
exam	fishing	pocket	children	rubbish

1. The ________ sit on the rocks.
2. I can go ________ at Tesco's.
3. The men went ________.
4. The ________ is at ten o'clock.
5. Beth was ________ when the rent went up.
6. The ________ can go in the bin.
7. Jeff will ________ his van.
8. I had a ________ for lunch.
9. I must go to the ________.
10. The man had a pen in his ________.

Choose a word from the box for each sentence:

collect	until	present	rabbit	attend
second	visit	spelling	public	padlock

1. I got a _________ for him at the shops.
2. Jack must _________ the dentist.
3. The _________ ran from the fox.
4. I will _________ the ten o'clock class.
5. The children had a _________ test.
6. Ali will _________ the TV from the shop.
7. I must get a _________ for the shed.
8. I will not sing in _________.
9. Sharon was _________ in the quiz.
10. I will not get a jacket _________ the spring.

Resource Book
Section Two

Dictation Sentences

There are 12 sentences for each of the main vowel phonemes.

They are in the order in which they are presented in the Extended Code of the Sounds~Write programme. They are found in Phases 3, 4 and 5 of Letters and Sounds. Only the more common ways of spelling the sounds are included.

'ae': <ai>, <ay>, <ea>, <ey>, <a-e>

'ee': <ee>, <ea>, <ie>, <y>, <e>

'oe': <oa>, <ow>, oe>, <o-e>, <o>

'er': <er>, <ir>, <ur>, <or>, <ear>

'e' : <e>, <ea>, <ai>

'ow': <ow>, <ou>

'oo'(as in moon) : <oo>, <ew>, <ue>, <u-e>, <ou>, <ough>

'ie' : <ie>, <i-e>, <igh>, <y>, <i>

'oo' (as in book) : <oo>, <u>, <oul>

'or' : <or>, <au>, <aw>, <al>, <a>, <oor>, <our>, <ore>, <ough>, <augh>

'air': <air>, <ere>, <ear>, <are>

'ar' : <ar>, <al>, <a>

The sentences only contain sounds learned up to that point.

Read the whole sentence and then repeat it slowly, saying one word at a time, while the learners write them down.

Dictate 1-3 sentences in a session, depending on the ability of the learners.

It is important that you hear the learners read the sentences on completion to give extra reading practice and to check for meaning and spelling.

Ideas for using these sentences for other activities can be found in the introduction to Dictation Sentences in Section One on pages 9 and 10

1. It may rain today.

2. That was a great game.

3. Jake will paint the gate.

4. The cat has a long tail.

5. I will bake a cake.

6. I had steak and chips.

7. The train was late.

8. They play a game of chess.

9. His name is Dave.

10. The chain may break.

11. There is not much rain in Spain.

12. I hate to get in late.

1. I am very happy.

2. He is the chief.

3. We eat meat on Sundays.

4. I will read that this week.

5. It is a sunny day.

6. I have big feet.

7. The sheep are in the field.

8. The sea is green.

9. I can see three trees.

10 He thinks she is funny.

11. A queen bee is very big.

12. Jean had cream cakes for tea.

1. I have a red coat.
2. She must go home.
3. Show me the old boat.
4. It may snow this week.
5. Joe had the most toast.
6. It is the only shop open.
7. Go slowly on this road.
8. We drove to the coast.
9. Show me the note.
10. He can make his boat float.
11. Joan will open the post.
12. The rose will grow.

1. The girl got hurt.
2. I must go to work.
3. It is cold in winter.
4. She turns left into her road.
5. Her skirt got dirty.
6. It is her third birthday.
7. The church is over the road.
8. Did she burn herself?
9. The earth turns on its axis.
10. The term ends on Thursday.
11. He sees his sister at work.
12. I must learn the words.

1. The old man is deaf.
2. Ben said he is ready.
3. I had egg on toast for breakfast.
4. Spread butter on the bread.
5. Jeff has a bad head.
6. I will mend it with this thread.
7. He said it again.
8. The bench was very heavy.
9. He left it in the shed.
10. We sweat in the hot weather.
11. She had a red hat on her head.
12. I was dealt a bad hand.

1. The old house was in town.

2. I found it on the ground.

3. I will count out loud.

4. The brown owl sat in a tree.

5. The dog growls at the postman.

6. The brown cows run round the field.

7. The mouse is on the ground.

8. The clown is funny.

9. We drove round town.

10. The black cloud is over our house.

11. The music is very loud.

12. I am about to go out.

1. The room is too big.
2. We flew to Spain.
3. Shall I give you a clue?
4. She had mushroom soup.
5. They will soon get proof.
6. The dog can jump through the hoop.
7. I will stick it with glue.
8. It will soon be June.
9. He grew big and strong.
10. Shall we paint the room blue?
11. It is rude to chew gum in class.
12. Sue has lots of food on her plate.

1. The child might cry.
2. Turn right at the lights.
3. The kind lady was shy.
4. I went by myself.
5. The moon was high in the sky.
6. He has nine ties.
7. She will try five times.
8. What time do we fly tonight?
9. You are quite right.
10. I like pie and chips.
11. Mike will ride his bike.
12. We will try to go higher.

1. Should I read this book?
2. The crook took the cash.
3. Let's look in the woods.
4. Would you cook dinner?
5. The children look at the books.
6. My bag is full.
7. Hang the coat on the hook.
8. He shook when the bull ran at him.
9. I am full after that pudding.
10. Should I push or pull?
11. He took his cap off the hook.
12. I took the book off the shelf.

1. It is always hot in August.

2. I will call for you at four o'clock.

3. We took straw for the horse.

4. He was born in August.

5. Paul is four today.

6. I saw him at the door.

7. I thought the child was naughty.

8. He taught my daughter.

9. The baby crawls on the floor.

10. The girl is short.

11. We will walk and talk.

12. We need more straws.

1. Sit on the chair over there.

2. I will wear my new dress.

3. I have fair hair.

4. How much is the bus fare?

5. Clare got a new pair of shoes.

6. Tear along the dotted line.

7. I dare not go near the bear.

8. Where are the stairs?

9. There are lots of chairs.

10. They dare not swear.

11. They share the pear.

12. I do not care if they stare.

1. Try to keep calm.
2. I will park the car in the car park.
3. The palm of my hand is sweaty.
4. Mark likes to play darts.
5. The stars are bright tonight.
6. Her father drove the car.
7. She looks very smart.
8. I start my new class next Friday.
9. Shall I ask for a jar of jam?
10. I got a card from my partner.
11. I love almond cake.
12. They put a plaster on her arm.

Picture-Word Matching

There is a page for each of the main vowel phonemes.

They are in the order in which they are presented in the Extended Code of the Sounds~Write programme. They are found in Phases 3, 4 and 5 of Letters and Sounds.

'ae' : <ai>, <ay>, <ea>, <a-e>

'ee' : <ee>, <ea>, <y>

'oe' : <oa>, <ow>, <oe>, <o-e>, <o>

'er' : <er>, <ir>, <ur>, <or>

'e' : <e>, <ea>

'ow' : <ow>, <ou>

'oo'(as in moon) : <oo>, <ew>, <ue>, <u-e>

'ie' : <ie>, <i-e>, <igh>, <y>, <i>

'oo' (as in book) : <oo>, <u>

'or' : <or>, <au>, <aw>, <al>, <a>, <oor>

'air' : <air>, <ere>, <ear>, <are>

'ar' : <ar>, <al>, <a>

Ask the learners to read a word from the box and find the picture to match. They then write the word next to the picture, saying the sounds as they write.

This is a useful exercise for ESOL or EAL learners, as it helps to increase their vocabulary.

Hear the learners read the words on completion, as extra reading practice.

The same words are used on the Gap-fill sheets. This enables the learners to have extra exposure to the words and to the different ways of spelling the target phoneme.

Match the words to the pictures:

tail	cake	wait	play	break
gate	paint	spray	train	plane

 ____________

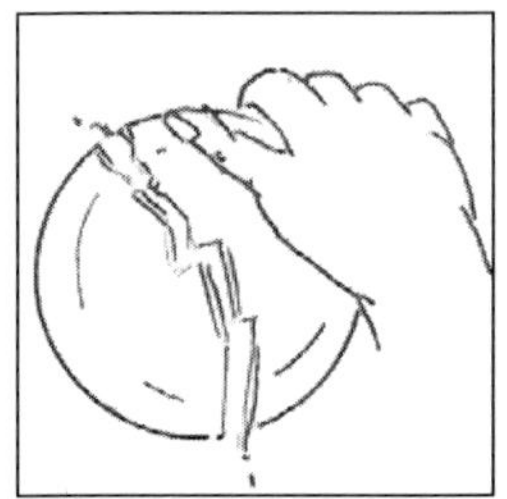 ____________

 ____________

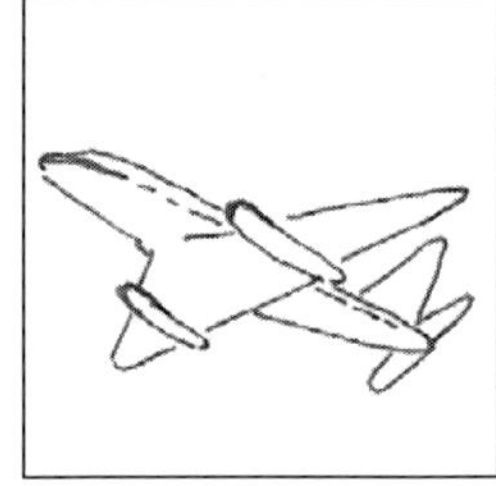 ____________

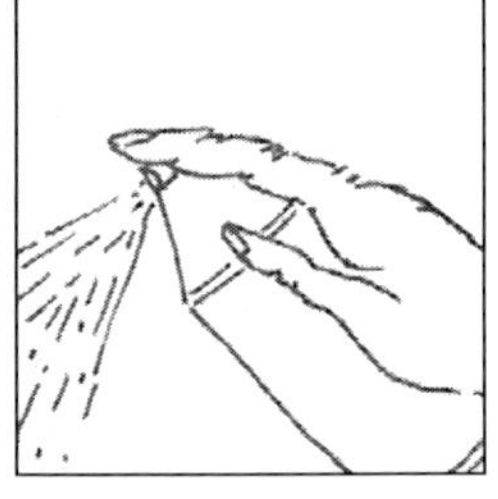 ____________

 ____________

 ____________

 ____________

 ____________

 ____________

Match the words to the pictures:

tea	baby	heel	sleep	seat
sunny	teeth	cheap	marry	three

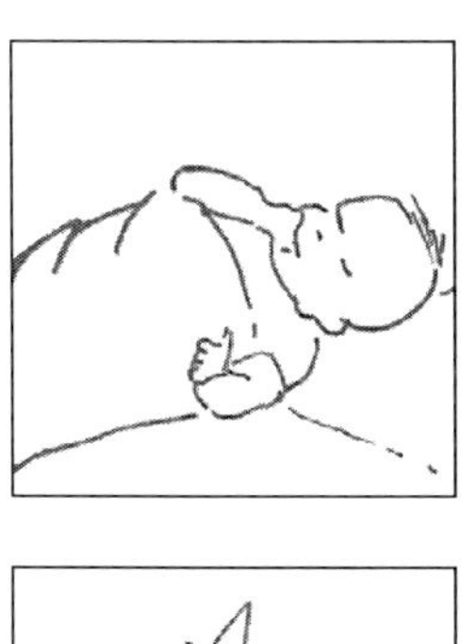 ______________

 ______________

____

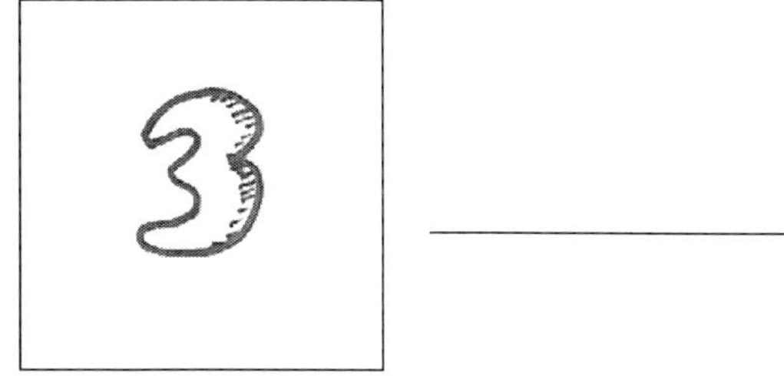 ______________

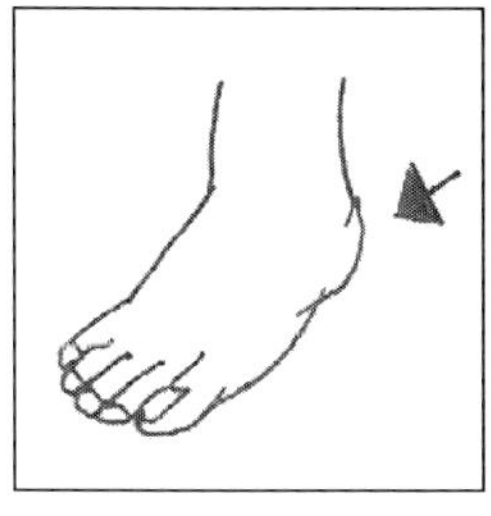 ______________

 ______________

 ______________

 ______________

 ______________

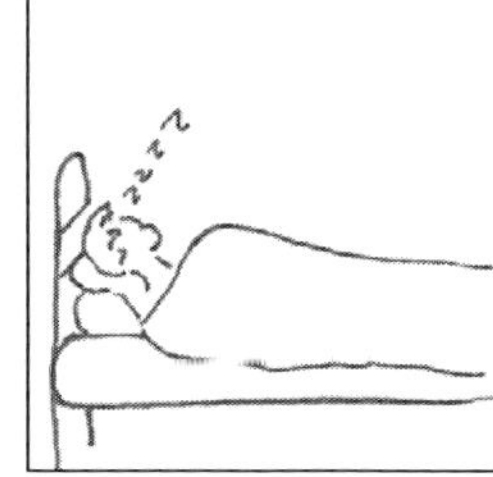 ______________

Match the words to the pictures:

blow	post	note	road	toe
toast	snow	grow	bone	old

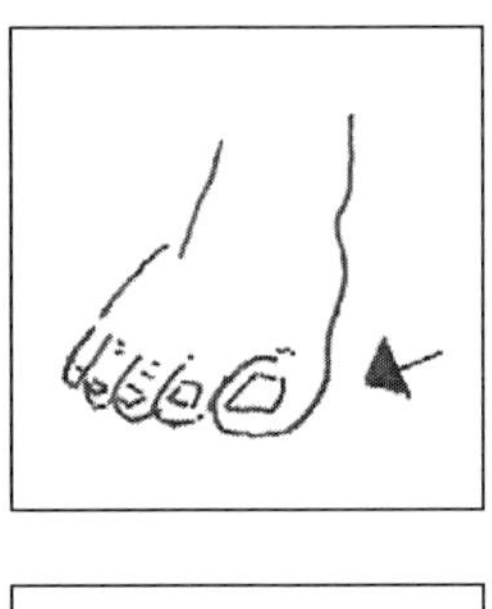

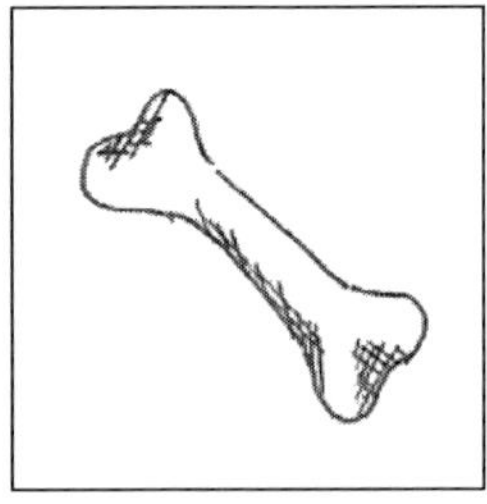

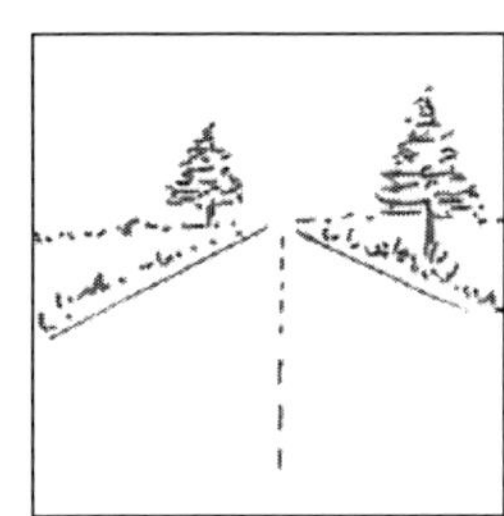

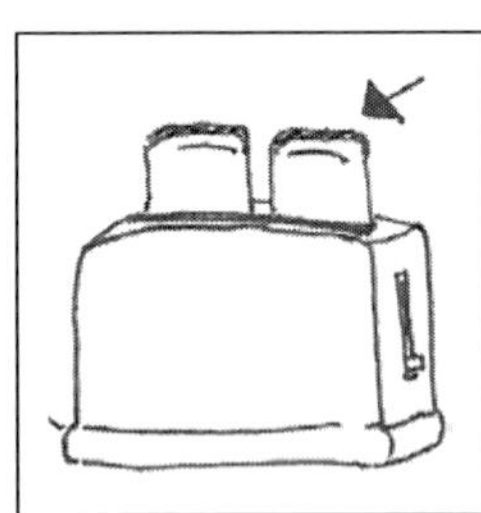

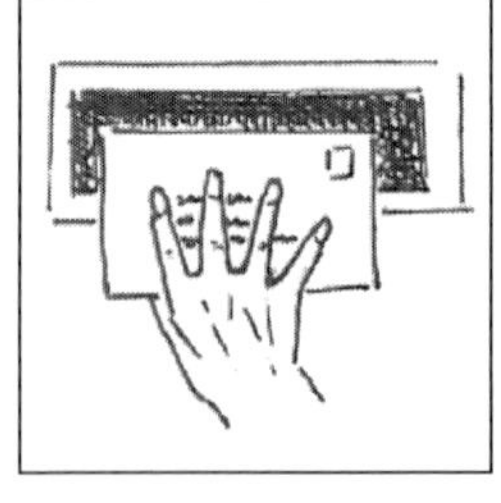

Match the words to the pictures:

shirt	summer	worm	turn	burger
doctor	Thursday	first	girl	sister

Match the words to the pictures:

bread	ten	thread	deaf	mend
ready	shed	spread	head	heavy

Match the words to the pictures:

mouth down owl cloud clown

shout house cow crowd count

Match the words to the pictures:

glue	June	spoon	grew	fruit
roof	flew	broom	food	rude

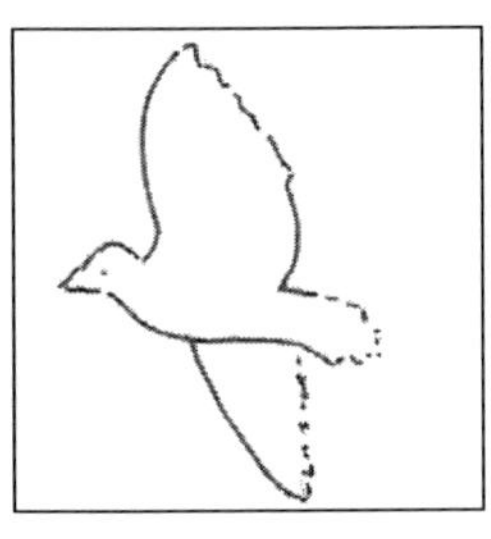 ____________

 ____________

 ____________

 ____________

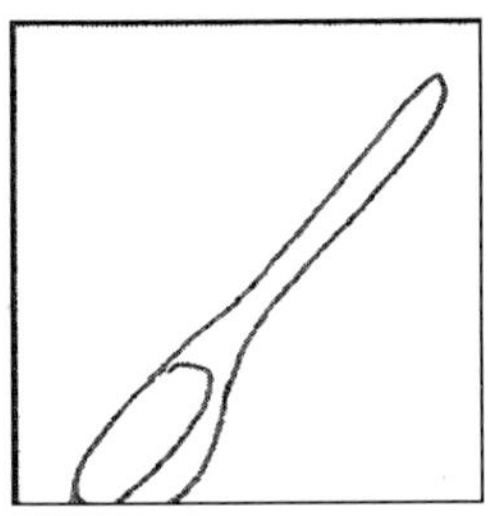 ____________

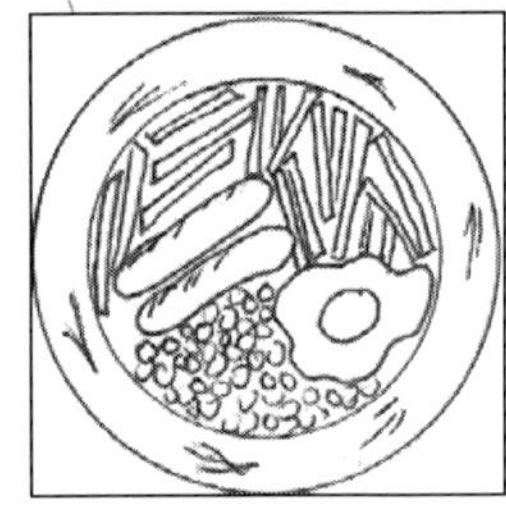 ____________

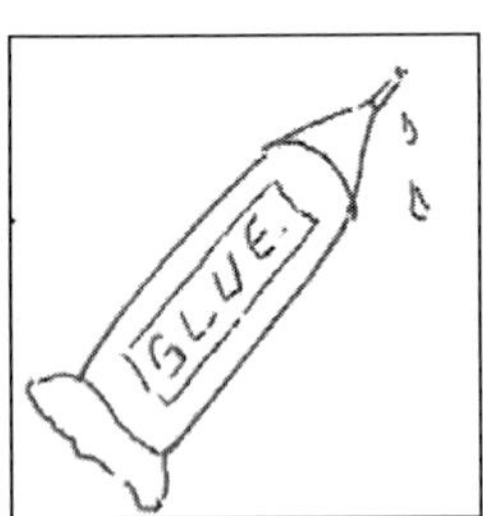

____

____

 ____________

 ____________

Match the words to the pictures:

bike	cry	light	lion	tie
tiger	fright	drive	lie	fly

Match the words to the pictures:

cook	put	hook	full	wood
look	full	foot	book	pull

Match the words to the pictures:

horse	ball	water	August	door
talk	walk	crawl	storm	saw

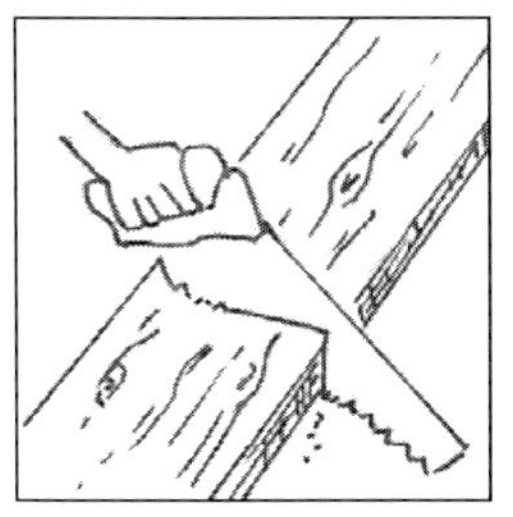 ______________

 ______________

 ______________

____

 ______________

 ______________

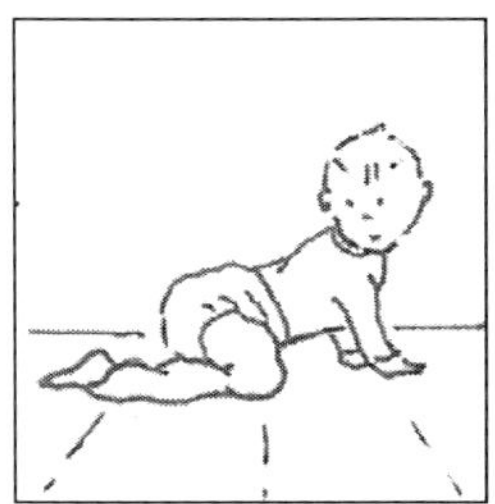 ______________

August

	2	9	16	23	30
	3	10	17	24	31
	4	11	18	25	
	5	12	19	26	
	6	13	20	27	
	7	14	21	28	
1	8	15	22	29	

____

 ______________

____

Match the words to the pictures:

chair	care	hair	tear	pear
there	stare	wear	bear	share

Match the words to the pictures:

car	tomato	bath	star	banana
half	March	palm	arm	glasses

Gap-Fills

There is a page for each of the main vowel phonemes.

They are in the order in which they are presented in the Extended Code of the Sounds~Write programme. They are found in Phases 3, 4 and 5 of Letters and Sounds.

Only the more common ways of spelling the sounds are included.

'ae' : <ai>, <ay>, <ea>, <a-e>

'ee' : <ee>, <ea>, <y>

'oe' : <oa>, <ow>, <oe>, <o-e>, <o>

'er' : <er>, <ir>, <ur>, <or>

'e' : <e>, <ea>

'ow' : <ow>, <ou>

'oo'(as in moon) : <oo>, <ew>, <ue>, <u-e>

'ie' : <ie>, <i-e>, <igh>, <y>, <i>

'oo' (as in book) : <oo>, <u>

'or' : <or>, <au>, <aw>, <al>, <a>, <oor>

'air' : <air>, <ere>, <ear>, <are>

'ar' : <ar>, <al>, <a>

The learners choose a word from the box to complete the sentences.

These are the same words that are used in the Picture-Word Matching exercise, so they become familiar to the learners. ESOL or EAL learners can refer to the pictures in order to understand their meaning. This helps them to learn new vocabulary and also to decide which word fits each sentence.

Choose a word from the box for each sentence:

tail	cake	wait	play	break
gate	paint	spray	train	plane

1. The children ______ in the sand.
2. A ______ runs on rails.
3. Ben will ______ the shed.
4. I will ______ for a bus.
5. I must shut the ______.
6. The ______ is on a plate.
7. I will stop for a ______.
8. The cat has a long ______.
9. The ______ was late.
10. I will ______ the paint.

Choose a word from the box for each sentence:

tea	baby	heel	sleep	seat
sunny	teeth	cheap	marry	three

1. We _______ in a bed.
2. The trainers are _______ in the sale.
3. I will make the _______.
4. It is a _______ day.
5. The _______ is in the cot.
6. Shall we sit on the _______?
7. They will _______ next May.
8. Tom has a pain in his _______.
9. I had _______ cakes for tea.
10. The man will clean his _______.

Choose a word from the box for each sentence:

blow	post	note	road	toe
toast	snow	grow	bone	old

1. The man trod on my ______.
2. I will cross the ______.
3. The dog ran away with the ______.
4. I will have a cup of tea and ______.
5. The ______ lady is eighty today.
6. Sam cannot play a ______ on his trumpet.
7. He will ______ big and strong.
8. She can open the ______.
9. I will ______ on my hot tea.
10. When it gets cold it may ______.

Choose a word from the box for each sentence:

shirt	summer	worm	turn	burger
doctor	Thursday	girl	sister	first

1. I had _______ and chips for dinner.
2. The bird ate the _______.
3. My _______ has long sleeves.
4. Nasreen was the _______ to finish her work.
5. Winter is cold but _______ is hot.
6. The _______ is thirteen on her birthday.
7. I got pills from the _______.
8. I need to _______ left to get to my house.
9. My _______ is thirty years old.
10. I have to go to the dentist next _______.

Choose a word from the box for each sentence:

bread	ten	thread	deaf	mend
ready	shed	spread	head	heavy

1. I must get a loaf of ______.
2. The hammer is in the ______.
3. We must get ______ to go on holiday.
4. The old lady was ______.
5. Ted can ______ the broken plate.
6. Jane will ______ butter on her toast.
7. Have you a hat to fit my big ______?
8. I will mend the coat with black ______.
9. The baby has ______ little toes.
10. The strong man can lift ______ weights.

Choose a word from the box for each sentence:

mouth	down	owl	cloud	clown
shout	house	cow	crowd	count

1. I live in a ______.

2. The black ______ will bring rain.

3. At the dentist I have to open my ______.

4. Jack can ______ up to ten.

5. The ______ sits in a tree.

6. We will go ______ the hill.

7. The ______ is in the field.

8. There was a big ______ at the match.

9. The ______ has a red nose.

10. I must not ______ at the children.

Choose a word from the box for each sentence:

glue	June	spoon	grew	fruit
roof	flew	rude	food	broom

1. The bird _______ into the tree.

2. We have a bowl of _______ on the table.

3. He will stick it on with _______.

4. We had lots of _______ for lunch.

5. We shall go on holiday in _______.

6. I will sweep up the mess with a _______.

7. The baby eats with a _______.

8. I _______ some flowers in a pot.

9. She was very _______ to her teacher.

10. The _______ of my house needs mending.

Choose a word from the box for each sentence:

bike	cry	light	lion	tie
tiger	lie	fright	drive	fly

1. He will ______ the bus up the hill.
2. I can ______ the fire when it gets cold.
3. That loud noise gave me a ______.
4. On Friday I will ride my ______ to work.
5. The birds ______ into the tree.
6. The ______ is fed at nine o'clock.
7. The sad film makes her ______.
8. I must have a ______ down on my bed.
9. The ______ is a wild animal.
10. She will ______ a ribbon on the present.

Choose a word from the box for each sentence:

cook	put	hook	full	wood
look	book	pull	foot	bull

1. I _______ out of the window.

2. Kim will _______ the cups away.

3. You could hang the coat on the _______.

4. A male cow is a _______.

5. Should I push or _______?

6. I could _______ lunch for you on Sunday.

7. We got lost in the _______.

8. She reads a _______ to the children.

9. The jug is _______ of milk.

10. He hurt his _______ when he fell.

Choose a word from the box for each sentence:

horse	ball	water	August	door
talk	walk	crawl	storm	saw

1. The boy lost his _______.
2. We will go on holiday in _______.
3. Jim went for a _______ in the sunshine.
4. The _______ is in the field.
5. Please close the _______ when you go out.
6. We must drink more _______ when it is hot.
7. We will _______ about it later.
8. The baby can _______ to the bedroom.
9. There was a bad _______ last night.
10. It is hard work to _______ the wood.

Choose a word from the box for each sentence:

chair	care	hair	tear	stare
there	pear	wear	bear	share

1. She will take _______ of the old lady.
2. I saw a _______ at the zoo.
3. Sit on the _______ next to me.
4. Be careful not to _______ the paper.
5. Jeff will _______ his best shirt.
6. Their house is over _______.
7. The children _______ the sweets.
8. Clare went to get her _______ cut.
9. Would you like an apple or a _______?
10. They _______ at the lady with purple hair.

Choose a word from the box for each sentence:

car	tomato	bath	star	banana
half	March	palm	arm	glasses

1. The _______ looks bright on a dark night.
2. I have only eaten _______ of my apple.
3. I like to have _______ soup for lunch.
4. I go into town in my _______.
5. The man wore _______ for reading.
6. ______ is the start of spring.
7. The boy hurt his _______ when he fell.
8. There is shade under the _______ tree.
9. We will get a new _______ in the bathroom.
10. There is one _______ left in the fruit bowl.

Word Analysis

Word analysis is a task that requires the learner to segment the words into separate phonemes. This is a particularly important skill for spelling.

There is a page for each of the main vowel phonemes.

They are in the order in which they are presented in the Sounds-Write programme. They are found in Phases 3, 4 and 5 of Letters and Sounds.

Only the more common ways of spelling the sounds are included. There are two sheets for the sound 'or' as it can be represented by so many different spellings.

'ae' : <ai>, <ay>, <ea>, <ey>, <a-e>

'ee' : <ee>, <ea>, <ey>, <y>, <e>

'oe' : <oa>, <ow>, <oe>, <o-e>, <o>

'er' : <er>, <ir>, <ur>, <or>, <ear>

'e' : <e>, <ea>, <ai>

'ow' : <ow>, <ou>

'oo'(as in moon) : <oo>, <ew>, <ue>, <u-e>, <ui>

'ie' : <ie>, <i-e>, <igh>, <y>, <i>

'oo' (as in book) : <oo>, <u>, <oul>

'or' (1) : <or>, <au>, <aw>, <al>, <a>, <ar>

'or' (2): <oor>, <oar>, <ore>, <our>, <ough>, <augh>

'air' : <air>, <ere>, <ear>, <are>

'ar' : <ar>, <al>, <a>

It is essential that the learners say the sounds as they underline them. This will help to establish the habit of saying the sounds as they write; a strategy which will lead to more accurate spelling.

There is a small line after each word on which the learners write the number of sounds in that word.

eg. r ai n 3
th ey 2
eigh t 2
b r ea k 4

Read each word. Say the sounds as you underline them.
Write the number of sounds on the line eg. r ai n 3

rain	__	late	__
tray	__	great	__
plate	__	play	__
day	__	gate	__
waist	__	brain	__
made	__	break	__
steak	__	train	__
nail	__	may	__

Read each word. Say the sounds as you underline them.
Write the number of sounds on the line eg. f ee t 3

feet	__	cream	__
happy	__	we	__
eat	__	funny	__
me	__	read	__
silly	__	tree	__
sweet	__	tea	__
she	__	sheet	__
meat	__	messy	__

Read each word. Say the sounds as you underline them.
Write the number of sounds on the line eg. c r ow 3

crow	__	cold	__
those	__	go	__
soak	__	bone	__
gold	__	toe	__
open	__	pole	__
cone	__	road	__
home	__	woke	__
throw	__	glow	__
coat	__	stroke	__

Read each word. Say the sounds as you underline them.
Write the number of sounds on the line eg. b ir d 3

bird	__	first	__
work	__	turn	__
burn	__	word	__
dirt	__	kerb	__
term	__	worst	__
shirt	__	girl	__
fur	__	world	__
her	__	winter	__

Read each word. Say the sounds as you underline them.
Write the number of sounds on the line eg. h ea d 3

head	__	deaf	__
then	__	again	__
dread	__	death	__
said	__	bench	__
dress	__	health	__
wealth	__	tent	__
spend	__	ready	__
chest	__	spread	__

Read each word. Say the sounds as you underline them.
Write the number of sounds on the line eg. l ou d 3

loud	__	proud	__
shout	__	crowd	__
cow	__	allow	__
sound	__	house	__
about	__	ground	__
brown	__	drown	__
found	__	now	__
town	__	owl	__
down	__	mouse	__

Read each word. Say the sounds as you underline them.
Write the number of sounds on the line eg. m oo n 3

moon __

June __

clue __

blue __

shoot __

to __

blew __

room __

chew __

flew __

spoon __

root __

rude __

true __

roof __

soon __

Read the word. Say the sounds as you underline them.
Write the number of sounds on the line eg. p ie 2

pie	__	light	__
try	__	cries	__
shine	__	child	__
tie	__	wife	__
wild	__	lie	__
night	__	my	__
sky	__	white	__
nine	__	right	__

Read each word. Say the sounds as you underline them.
Write the number of sounds on the line eg. b oo k 3

book	__	should	__
pull	__	bush	__
could	__	hook	__
look	__	put	__
cook	__	shook	__
would	__	push	__
full	__	wool	__
wood	__	crook	__

Read the word. Say the sounds as you underline them.
Write the number of sounds on the line eg. f or k 3

fork	__	warm	__
draw	__	born	__
saw	__	walk	__
hall	__	storm	__
August	__	horse	__
crawl	__	short	__
small	__	awful	__
talk	__	call	__

Read each word. Say the sounds as you underline them.
Write the number of sounds on the line eg. f our 2

four __	brought __
more __	caught __
board __	door __
taught __	roar __
thought __	naughty __
score __	poor __
pour __	snore __
daughter __	floor __

Read each word. Say the sounds as you underline them.
Write the number of sounds on the line eg. ch air 2

chair	__	pear	__
stare	__	stair	__
there	__	air	__
hair	__	wear	__
care	__	fair	__
swear	__	bear	__
their	__	glare	__
share	__	where	__

Read each word. Say the sounds as you underline them.
Write the number of sounds on the line eg. c ar 2

car	__	glass	__
start	__	laugh	__
father	__	after	__
half	__	far	__
sharp	__	ask	__
class	__	smart	__
calm	__	bath	__
card	__	charge	__

Wordsearches

This is a useful exercise to be given at the end of a class or as homework. Its purpose is to give extra reading practice, as well as being fun. However, be aware that wordsearches can be completed without it being necessary to read the words! It is important, therefore, to hear the learner read the words to you on completion of the wordsearch.

There is a wordsearch for each of the main vowel phonemes.

These are in the order in which they are presented in the Extended Code of the Sounds~Write programme. They are found in Phases 3, 4 and 5 of Letters and Sounds.

Only the more common ways of spelling the sounds are included. There are two sheets for the sound 'or' as it can be represented by so many different spellings.

'ae' : <ai>, <ay>, <ea>, <ey>, <a-e>

'ee' : <ee>, <ea>, <ey>, <y>, <e>

'oe' : <oa>, <ow>, <oe>, <o-e>, <o>

'er' : <er>, <ir>, <ur>, <or>, <ear>

'e' : <e>, <ea>, <ai>

'ow' : <ow>, <ou>

'oo'(as in moon) : <oo>, <ew>, <ue>, <u-e>, <ui>

'ie' : <ie>, <i-e>, <igh>, <y>, <i>

'oo' (as in book) : <oo>, <u>, <oul>

'or' (1) : <or>, <au>, <aw>, <al>, <a>, <ar>

'or' (2): <oor>, <oar>, <ore>, <our>, <ough>, <augh>

'air' : <air>, <ere>, <ear>, <are>

'ar' : <ar>, <al>, <a>

f	d	e	b	j	g	r	e	a	t
k	i	y	r	s	w	b	v	m	h
c	a	m	e	x	n	t	a	k	e
h	t	e	a	s	g	j	m	o	y
a	z	c	k	u	s	t	a	y	r
i	w	b	r	i	l	r	x	h	u
n	a	m	e	z	h	a	y	e	d
a	g	i	k	r	a	i	n	v	a
l	y	e	w	z	b	n	m	h	t
d	a	y	c	j	y	o	e	s	e

Find these words:

name	stay
train	take
date	rain
they	day
break	great
chain	came

i	s	u	n	n	y	f	h	j	h
g	b	y	w	e	s	x	t	k	a
r	z	v	c	h	e	a	p	m	p
e	d	j	n	u	a	t	h	i	p
a	s	f	c	v	t	o	p	k	y
d	r	e	a	m	r	j	w	l	c
x	b	e	n	u	t	w	e	e	k
s	c	t	b	s	m	p	k	y	e
d	h	j	o	h	v	x	m	l	y
a	t	r	e	e	f	u	b	e	x

Find these words:

week	happy
eat	key
read	tree
sunny	feet
she	cheap
dream	we

u	g	l	e	w	a	b	o	a	t
m	o	s	t	b	x	i	y	p	o
z	v	d	n	k	s	f	b	u	e
c	p	e	r	o	a	d	s	x	n
o	x	t	j	p	k	o	r	d	g
l	w	f	g	e	j	l	y	a	s
d	x	s	c	n	o	t	e	v	h
m	u	l	r	v	j	k	p	i	o
b	c	o	a	t	n	y	t	d	m
v	t	w	y	k	b	h	o	l	e

Find these words:

boat	road
home	cold
slow	most
coat	note
open	hole
toe	go

w	r	l	u	s	i	s	t	e	r
d	a	e	x	v	j	k	u	l	o
s	t	a	w	c	e	a	r	t	h
f	i	r	s	t	z	m	n	y	u
r	g	n	k	e	o	p	s	w	r
h	y	v	s	r	k	r	b	l	t
w	o	r	d	m	x	n	i	j	y
o	s	t	h	e	g	i	r	l	w
r	z	n	r	u	d	j	d	m	k
k	e	x	t	w	i	n	t	e	r

Find these words:

earth	winter
sister	first
learn	turn
term	work
bird	girl
word	hurt

c	t	h	r	e	a	d	u	x	w
s	h	g	i	b	g	o	s	p	a
h	e	a	d	y	a	d	a	h	s
f	n	p	w	z	i	n	i	k	p
m	y	r	s	c	n	t	d	m	r
s	h	e	d	o	y	w	l	p	e
w	x	f	e	n	u	t	m	e	a
e	k	l	a	r	b	r	e	a	d
a	s	w	f	m	o	z	n	p	t
t	d	v	g	r	e	a	d	y	k

Find these words:

mend	head
said	then
shed	deaf
ready	again
bread	sweat
spread	thread

p	n	o	w	x	h	o	u	s	e
r	s	h	y	c	j	k	a	h	x
o	l	b	i	f	r	u	m	o	b
u	x	r	g	u	h	c	k	u	e
n	s	o	v	a	b	o	u	t	n
d	o	w	n	j	l	u	r	s	x
v	h	n	y	l	e	n	k	l	a
r	e	y	f	o	h	t	o	w	n
m	c	g	r	u	k	i	w	f	z
f	o	u	n	d	c	h	l	n	o

Find these words:

now	owl
down	loud
count	town
found	house
brown	round
about	shout

f	r	u	i	t	x	s	u	i	t
s	u	b	o	p	r	p	w	a	r
v	d	z	s	m	o	o	n	k	u
j	e	t	e	l	y	o	u	d	e
g	s	c	b	r	f	n	l	n	o
r	o	o	f	p	t	w	z	d	c
e	j	v	l	k	r	l	g	k	h
w	i	d	e	v	x	b	l	u	e
b	k	o	w	h	m	y	r	d	w
z	b	t	g	k	r	o	o	m	l

Find these words:

room rude

chew grew

blue moon

suit roof

flew true

spoon fruit

w	t	i	m	e	d	x	f	l	y
s	i	f	y	h	k	j	z	m	o
g	e	r	y	j	c	h	i	l	d
x	d	n	b	n	o	u	t	i	e
d	r	i	v	e	s	e	w	g	p
z	v	g	k	u	t	d	k	h	i
k	s	h	i	g	h	w	a	t	j
i	m	t	c	b	n	u	p	s	l
n	r	y	o	c	x	a	h	k	i
d	t	l	w	i	f	e	b	m	e

Find these words:

fly
lie
kind
night
drive
high
tie
my
time
child
light
wife

w	o	u	l	d	z	f	u	l	l
h	g	r	o	w	l	j	y	n	v
s	e	c	o	o	k	h	p	u	i
z	b	f	k	y	d	k	b	c	t
p	u	t	d	e	s	h	o	o	k
u	s	c	r	g	h	m	i	u	g
l	z	r	b	o	o	k	n	l	u
l	w	j	u	y	u	z	t	d	f
j	i	h	s	o	l	e	s	b	n
p	u	s	h	c	d	u	k	v	w

Find these words:

full
book
cook
put
push
pull
shook
bush
would
look
should
could

s	m	a	l	l	e	d	y	s	k
a	j	x	d	r	h	r	l	b	t
w	a	r	m	s	n	a	z	o	p
b	c	f	u	o	g	w	a	r	d
a	w	d	r	a	v	o	m	n	e
u	s	c	t	h	j	i	b	d	x
t	d	o	v	m	f	a	u	l	t
h	o	r	s	e	z	b	r	w	a
o	s	k	h	u	v	c	o	n	l
r	f	y	b	p	s	t	a	l	k

Find these words:

horse	small
stalk	cork
author	fault
draw	talk
born	ward
warm	saw

d	a	u	g	h	t	e	r	i	t
o	x	b	m	u	l	j	w	a	h
o	d	s	o	r	e	h	z	v	o
r	y	u	k	w	f	n	b	j	u
s	w	f	x	c	b	k	o	y	g
p	o	o	r	s	o	r	u	l	h
o	h	u	z	t	a	u	g	h	t
u	c	r	o	a	r	y	h	m	v
r	d	t	h	y	d	x	t	r	o
v	w	o	r	e	m	t	e	k	p

Find these words:

board
daughter
wore
bought
four
pour
roar
sore
poor
thought
taught
door

w	e	a	r	x	c	h	a	i	r
z	g	t	j	b	a	d	i	k	p
v	s	i	f	l	r	w	r	m	u
c	w	h	e	r	e	o	y	e	h
n	e	t	d	s	u	t	k	j	b
h	a	i	r	x	s	h	a	r	e
b	r	g	y	n	f	e	h	s	a
v	p	j	p	a	i	r	c	t	r
w	h	c	i	s	k	e	y	z	l
d	a	r	e	x	u	h	n	e	d

Find these words:

where	swear
share	chair
pair	care
bear	there
air	hair
wear	dare

s	m	a	r	t	j	s	y	o	a
t	d	l	h	g	p	t	c	w	b
a	i	m	e	s	z	a	s	k	v
r	t	o	x	c	a	r	p	m	f
t	b	n	e	a	y	w	g	u	a
i	l	d	a	r	t	s	e	w	t
c	k	m	v	d	y	m	h	d	h
a	w	r	x	u	k	b	a	t	e
l	a	u	g	h	s	e	l	j	r
m	k	z	b	o	t	w	f	k	c

Find these words:

father	almond
start	smart
calm	half
card	star
dart	laugh
ask	car

Spelling

There are two pages for each of the main vowel phonemes.

They are in the order in which they are presented in the Extended Code of the Sounds~Write programme. They can be found in Phases 3, 4 and 5 of Letters and Sounds.

Only the more common ways of spelling the sounds are included. There are two sheets for the sound 'or' as it can be represented by so many different spellings.

'ae' : <ai>, <ay>, <ea>, <ey>, <a-e>

'ee' : <ee>, <ea>, <ey>, <y>, <e>

'oe' : <oa>, <ow>, <oe>, <o-e>, <o>

'er' : <er>, <ir>, <ur>, <or>, <ear>

'e' : <e>, <ea>, <ai>

'ow' : <ow>, <ou>

'oo'(as in moon) : <oo>, <ew>, <ue>, <u-e>, <ui>

'ie' : <ie>, <i-e>, <igh>, <y>, <i>

'oo' (as in book) : <oo>, <u>, <oul>

'or' (1) : <or>, <au>, <aw>, <al>, <a>, <ar>

'or' (2): <oor>, <oar>, <ore>, <our>, <ough>, <augh>

'air' : <air>, <ere>, <ear>, <are>

'ar' : <ar>, <al>, <a>

There are two different sheets, which enable the following versions:

One syllable words only (half sheet)

One syllable words with a sorting activity.

Two syllable words only (half sheet)

One and two syllable words on one sheet for learners at this level.

One page contains 10 one-syllable words and 10 two-syllable words. The page can be given to the learners, as it is, if they can cope with so much at once. For some learners, that might be too challenging, so the page can be cut in half, so that only one-syllable words are given at first and two syllables at a later date.

The other sheet is the one-syllable words accompanied by a sorting activity. Categorising helps learning – so the act of sorting the words by identifying the different graphemes used to represent that phoneme, will aid memory.

The layout of the sheets is similar to the Look – Read – Cover – Write strategy that has been in vogue for many years. However, that method relied on visual memorisation. This is in conflict with current thinking. We now approach reading and spelling by identifying the sounds in words and relating them to the symbols we use to represent those sounds. So there is a fundamental difference in the approach to these pages.

Think of the mnemonic – **R-A-P**

Read

Analyse

Practise

Analyse being the added extra and the most important activity.

The learners should be instructed to read the word and then segment it by saying the separate sounds as they underline them eg. f ee t. They say the sounds again as they write them on the lines provided eg. _ __ _. There are two further lines for them to practise writing the word, always saying the sounds as they write.

It is essential to teach the learners to complete this task correctly, in order to achieve optimum benefit. It is more about teaching an approach to spelling than learning to spell those particular words.

In order to spell accurately, the learner needs to be able to segment the word into separate sounds and then write a symbol to represent each sound. The complication in English is that we have different ways to spell the sounds, so underlining each grapheme will help the learner notice the composition of the words. Encourage them to consciously notice how the target phoneme is represented in each word eg. feet, eat, happy . It might help if they underline or highlighting that grapheme in another colour. This will make it more visual, clearly identifying it and aiding recall.

Underline the sounds in each word. Then write them and say the sounds as you go.

day _ __ ________ ________

break _ _ __ _ ________ ________

rain _ __ _ ________ ________

say _ __ ________ ________

take _ _ _ _ ________ ________

great _ _ __ _ ________ ________

stay _ _ __ ________ ________

train _ _ __ _ ________ ________

made _ _ _ _ ________ ________

pain _ __ _ ________ ________

Sort the words into the different spellings for 'ae':

ay	ai
ea	**a-e**

Underline the sounds in each word. Then write them and say the sounds as you go.

she	__ _	________	________
week	_ __ _	________	________
seat	_ __ _	________	________
see	_ __	________	________
these	__ _ _ _	________	________
dream	_ _ __ _	________	________
happy	_ _ __ _	________	________
me	_ _	________	________
sunny	_ _ __ _	________	________
eat	__ _	________	________

Sort the words into the different spellings for 'ee':

ee	e
ea	**y**

Underline the sounds in each word. Then write them and say the sounds as you go.

home _ _ _ _ ________ ________
slow _ _ _ ________ ________
old _ _ _ ________ ________
road _ _ _ ________ ________
show _ _ ________ ________
bone _ _ _ _ ________ ________
boat _ _ _ ________ ________
grow _ _ _ ________ ________
toe _ _ ________ ________
most _ _ _ _ ________ ________

Sort the words into the different spellings for 'oe':

ow	o	o-e	oa	oe

Underline the sounds in each word. Then write them and say the sounds as you go.

first _ _ _ _ ____________ ____________

her _ _ ____________ ____________

work _ _ _ ____________ ____________

earn _ _ ____________ ____________

turn _ _ _ ____________ ____________

shirt _ _ _ ____________ ____________

term _ _ _ ____________ ____________

word _ _ _ ____________ ____________

learn _ _ _ ____________ ____________

hurt _ _ _ ____________ ____________

Sort the words into the different spellings for 'er':

er	ur	ir	or	ear

Underline the sounds in each word. Then write them and say the sounds as you go.

head _ __ _ ____________ ____________

best _ _ _ _ ____________ ____________

deaf _ __ _ ____________ ____________

shed __ _ _ ____________ ____________

bread _ _ __ _ ____________ ____________

meant _ __ _ _ ____________ ____________

send _ _ _ _ ____________ ____________

said _ __ _ ____________ ____________

thread __ _ __ _ ____________ ____________

spread _ _ _ __ _ ____________ ____________

Sort the words into the different spellings for 'e':

e	ea	ai

Underline the sounds in each word. Then write them and say the sounds as you go.

down _ __ _ ________ ________

house _ __ __ ________ ________

now _ __ ________ ________

found _ __ _ _ ________ ________

brown _ _ __ _ ________ ________

out __ _ ________ ________

how _ __ ________ ________

ground _ _ __ _ _ ________ ________

our __ _ ________ ________

town _ __ _ ________ ________

Sort the words into the different spellings for 'ow':

ow	ou

Underline the sounds in each word. Then write them and say the sounds as you go.

chew __ __ ____________ ____________

suit _ __ _ ____________ ____________

blue _ _ __ ____________ ____________

grew _ _ __ ____________ ____________

food _ __ _ ____________ ____________

true _ _ __ ____________ ____________

June _ _ _ _ ____________ ____________

room _ __ _ ____________ ____________

fruit _ _ __ _ ____________ ____________

rude _ _ _ _ ____________ ____________

Sort the words into the different spellings for 'oo':

oo	ue	u-e	ew	ui

Underline the sounds in each word. Then write them and say the sounds as you go.

time _ _ _ _ ______ ______

my _ _ ______ ______

mind _ _ _ _ ______ ______

night _ ___ _ ______ ______

try _ _ _ ______ ______

while _ _ _ _ ______ ______

child _ _ _ _ ______ ______

might _ ___ _ ______ ______

pie _ _ ______ ______

drive _ _ _ _ _ ______ ______

Sort the words into the different spellings for 'ie':

ie	i-e	igh	y	i

Underline the sounds in each word. Then write them and say the sounds as you go.

good _ __ _ __________ __________

could _ ___ _ __________ __________

put _ _ _ __________ __________

would _ ___ _ __________ __________

cook _ __ _ __________ __________

push _ _ __ __________ __________

should __ ___ _ __________ __________

look _ __ _ __________ __________

full _ _ __ __________ __________

took _ __ _ __________ __________

Sort the words into the different spellings for 'oo':

oo	u	oul

Underline the sounds in each word. Then write them and say the sounds as you go.

for _ __ __________ __________

saw _ __ __________ __________

warm _ __ _ __________ __________

all _ __ __________ __________

draw _ _ __ __________ __________

short __ __ _ __________ __________

fault _ __ _ _ __________ __________

war _ __ __________ __________

call _ _ __ __________ __________

walk _ __ _ __________ __________

Sort the words into the different spellings for 'or':

aw	or	au
a	**al**	**ar**

Underline the sounds in each word. Then write them and say the sounds as you go.

door _ ___ ____________ ____________

more _ ___ ____________ ____________

roar _ ___ ____________ ____________

bought _ ______ _ ____________ ____________

score _ _ ___ ____________ ____________

four _ ___ ____________ ____________

floor _ _ ___ ____________ ____________

board _ ____ _ ____________ ____________

pour _ ____ ____________ ____________

caught _ ____ _ ____________ ____________

Sort the words into the different spellings for 'or':

ore	oor	oar
our	**ough**	**augh**

Underline the sounds in each word. Then write them and say the sounds as you go.

there __ ___ ______ ______

chair __ ___ ______ ______

rare _ ___ ______ ______

hair _ ___ ______ ______

where __ ___ ______ ______

scare _ _ ___ ______ ______

wear _ ___ ______ ______

care _ ___ ______ ______

pear _ ___ ______ ______

stair _ _ ___ ______ ______

Sort the words into the different spellings for 'air':

air	ere
are	**ear**

Underline the sounds in each word. Then write them and say the sounds as you go.

car _ __ ____________ ____________

half _ __ _ ____________ ____________

start _ _ __ _ ____________ ____________

park _ __ _ ____________ ____________

calm _ __ _ ____________ ____________

dance _ _ _ __ ____________ ____________

staff _ _ _ __ ____________ ____________

card _ __ _ ____________ ____________

ask _ _ _ ____________ ____________

bath _ _ __ ____________ ____________

Sort the words into the different spellings for 'ar':

ar	a	al

Underline the sounds in each word. Then write them and say the sounds as you go.

day	_ __	________	________
break	_ _ __ _	________	________
rain	_ __ _	________	________
say	_ __	________	________
take	_ _ _ _	________	________
great	_ _ __ _	________	________
stay	_ _ __	________	________
train	_ _ __ _	________	________
made	_ _ _ _	________	________
pain	_ __ _	________	________

2 syllables

a/way	_/_ __	________	________
con/tain	_ _ _/_ __ _	________	________
dis/play	_ _ _/_ _ __	________	________
mis/take	_ _ _/_ _ _ _	________	________
Sun/day	_ _ _/_ __	________	________
rail/way	_ __ _/_ __	________	________
ba/sic	_ _/_ _ _	________	________
pain/less	_ __ _/_ _ __	________	________
A/pril	_/_ _ __	________	________
a/fraid	_/_ _ __ _	________	________

Underline the sounds in each word. Then write them and say the sounds as you go.

she	__ _	________	________
week	_ __ _	________	________
seat	_ __ _	________	________
see	_ __	________	________
happy	_ _ __ _	________	________
dream	_ _ __ _	________	________
three	__ _ __	________	________
me	_ _	________	________
sunny	_ _ __ _	________	________
eat	__ _	________	________

2 syllables

ha/ppy	_ _/__ _	________	________
six/teen	_ _ _/_ __ _	________	________
begin	_ _ /_ _ _	________	________
rea/son	_ __/_ _ _	________	________
co/ffee	_ _ /__ __	________	________
week/end	_ __ _/_ _ _	________	________
ex/treme	_ _/_ _ _ _ _	________	________
ve/ry	_ _/_ _	________	________
a/gree	_/_ _ __	________	________
be/tween	_ _/_ _ __ _	________	________

Underline the sounds in each word. Then write them and say the sounds as you go.

home
slow
old
road
show
bone
boat
grow
toe
most

2 syllables

a/pproach
win/dow
post/code
snow/ing
bo/rrow
pot/hole
yell/ow
go/ing
re/mote
cross/road

Underline the sounds in each word. Then write them and say the sounds as you go.

first	_ __ _ _	________	________
her	_ __	________	________
work	_ __ _	________	________
earn	___ _	________	________
turn	_ __ _	________	________
shirt	__ __ _	________	________
term	_ __ _	________	________
word	_ __ _	________	________
learn	_ ___ _	________	________
hurt	_ __ _	________	________

2 syllables

dinn/er	_ _ __/__	________	________
ne/ver	_ _/_ __	________	________
Thurs/day	__ __ _/_ __	________	________
birth/day	_ __ __/_ __	________	________
sis/ter	_ _ _/_ __	________	________
thir/ty	__ __/_ _	________	________
ear/ly	___/_ _	________	________
re/turn	_ _/_ __ _	________	________
af/ter	_ _/_ __	________	________
search/ing	_ ___ __/_ __	________	________

Underline the sounds in each word. Then write them and say the sounds as you go.

head _ __ _ ________ ________

best _ _ _ _ ________ ________

deaf _ __ _ ________ ________

shed __ _ _ ________ ________

bread _ _ __ _ ________ ________

meant _ __ _ _ ________ ________

send _ _ _ _ ________ ________

said _ __ _ ________ ________

thread __ _ __ _ ________ ________

spread _ _ _ __ _ ________ ________

2 syllables

a/gain _ /_ __ _ ________ ________

ma/ny _ _ /_ _ ________ ________

a/ttend _ /__ _ _ _ ________ ________

den/tist _ _ _/_ _ _ _ ________ ________

ab/sent _ _ /_ _ _ _ ________ ________

a/gainst _ /_ __ _ _ _ ________ ________

break/fast _ _ __ _/_ _ _ _ ________ ________

help/less _ _ _ _/_ _ __ ________ ________

head/lamp _ __ _/_ _ _ _ ________ ________

health/y _ __ _ __/_ ________ ________

Underline the sounds in each word. Then write them and say the sounds as you go.

down _ __ _ ________ ________

house _ __ __ ________ ________

now _ __ ________ ________

found _ __ _ _ ________ ________

brown _ _ __ _ ________ ________

out __ _ ________ ________

how _ __ ________ ________

ground _ _ __ _ _ ________ ________

our __ _ ________ ________

town _ __ _ ________ ________

2 syllables

a/round _/_ __ _ _ ________ ________

count/y _ __ _ _/ _ ________ ________

a/llow _/__ __ ________ ________

a/bout _/_ __ _ ________ ________

moun/tain _ __ _/_ __ _ ________ ________

count/ing _ __ _ _/_ __ ________ ________

down/load _ __ _/_ __ _ ________ ________

cloud/y _ _ __ _/_ ________ ________

su/rround _ _/__ __ _ _ ________ ________

a/loud _/_ __ _ ________ ________

Underline the sounds in each word. Then write them and say the sounds as you go.

chew

suit

blue

grew

food

true

June

room

fruit

rude

2 syllables

bed/room

fool/ish

in/clude

ba/lloon

to/day

su/per

blue/bell

tea/spoon

suit/case

sham/poo

Underline the sounds in each word. Then write them and say the sounds as you go.

time _ _ _ _ ________ ________
my _ _ ________ ________
mind _ _ _ _ ________ ________
night _ ___ _ ________ ________
try _ _ _ ________ ________
while _ _ _ _ ________ ________
child _ _ _ _ ________ ________
might _ ___ _ ________ ________
pie _ __ ________ ________
drive _ _ _ _ _ ________ ________

2 syllables

day/light _ __/_ ___ _ ________ ________
be/hind _ _/_ _ _ _ ________ ________
my/self _ _/_ _ _ _ ________ ________
de/cide _ _/_ _ _ _ ________ ________
fi/nal _ _/_ __ ________ ________
to/night _ _/_ ___ _ ________ ________
Ju/ly _ _/_ _ ________ ________
nine/teen _ _ _ _/_ __ _ ________ ________
dis/like _ _ _/_ _ _ _ ________ ________
Fri/day _ _ _/_ __ ________ ________

Underline the sounds in each word. Then write them and say the sounds as you go.

good _ __ _ ________ ________

could _ ___ _ ________ ________

put _ _ _ ________ ________

would _ ___ _ ________ ________

cook _ __ _ ________ ________

push _ _ __ ________ ________

should __ ___ _ ________ ________

look _ __ _ ________ ________

full _ _ __ ________ ________

took _ __ _ ________ ________

2 syllables

book/shop _ __ _/__ _ _ ________ ________

thankful __ _ _ _/_ _ _ ________ ________

pull/ing _ _ __/_ __ ________ ________

cook/er _ __ _/__ ________ ________

grate/ful _ _ _ _ _/_ _ _ ________ ________

pain/ful _ __ _/_ _ _ ________ ________

crook/ed _ _ __ _/_ _ ________ ________

could/n't _ ___ _/_'_ ________ ________

look/ing _ __ _/_ __ ________ ________

wood/work _ __ _/_ __ _ ________ ________

Underline the sounds in each word. Then write them and say the sounds as you go.

for	_ __	________	________
saw	_ __	________	________
warm	_ __ _	________	________
all	_ __	________	________
draw	_ _ __	________	________
short	__ __ _	________	________
fault	_ __ _ _	________	________
war	_ __	________	________
call	_ _ __	________	________
walk	_ __ _	________	________

2 syllables

aw/ful	__/_ _ _	________	________
draw/ing	_ _ __/_ __	________	________
foot/ball	_ __ _/_ _ __	________	________
morn/ing	_ __ _/_ __	________	________
corn/er	_ __ _/__	________	________
al/so	_ _/_ _	________	________
re/ward	_ _/_ __ _	________	________
for/get	_ __/_ _ _	________	________
Au/gust	__/_ _ _ _	________	________
a/fford	_/__ __ _	________	________

Underline the sounds in each word. Then write them and say the sounds as you go.

door _ ___ ________ ________

more _ ___ ________ ________

roar _ ___ ________ ________

bought _ ___ _ ________ ________

score _ _ ___ ________ ________

four _ ___ ________ ________

floor _ _ ___ ________ ________

board _ ___ _ ________ ________

pour _ ___ ________ ________

caught _ ___ _ ________ ________

2 syllables

be/fore _ _/_ ___ ________ ________

door/way _ ___/_ __ ________ ________

snow/board _ _ __/_ ___ _ ________ ________

pour/ing _ ___/_ __ ________ ________

thought/ful __ ___ _/_ _ _ ________ ________

naugh/ty _ ___/_ _ ________ ________

ig/nore _ _/ _ ___ ________ ________

score/board _ _ ___/_ ___ _ ________ ________

daugh/ter _ ___/_ __ ________ ________

floor/ing _ _ ___/_ __ ________ ________

Underline the sounds in each word. Then write them and say the sounds as you go.

there __ ___ ________ ________

chair __ ___ ________ ________

rare _ ___ ________ ________

hair _ ___ ________ ________

where __ ___ ________ ________

scare _ _ ___ ________ ________

fair _ ___ ________ ________

care _ ___ ________ ________

pear _ ___ ________ ________

stair _ _ ___ ________ ________

2 syllables

air/port ___ /_ __ _ ________ ________

be/ware _ _/_ ___ ________ ________

care/ful _ ___/_ _ _ ________ ________

re/pair _ _ /_ ___ ________ ________

stair/case _ _ ___/_ _ _ _ ________ ________

chair/man _ ___/_ _ _ ________ ________

night/mare _ ___ _/_ ___ ________ ________

air/mail ___/_ __ _ ________ ________

wear/ing _ ___/_ __ ________ ________

there/fore __ ___ /_ ___ ________ ________

Underline the sounds in each word. Then write them and say the sounds as you go.

car _ __ ________ ________

half _ __ _ ________ ________

start _ _ __ _ ________ ________

park _ __ _ ________ ________

calm _ __ _ ________ ________

dance _ _ _ __ ________ ________

staff _ _ _ __ ________ ________

card _ __ _ ________ ________

ask _ _ _ ________ ________

bath _ _ __ ________ ________

2 syllables

fa/ther _ _/__ __ ________ ________

par/don _ __/_ _ _ ________ ________

al/mond __/_ _ _ _ ________ ________

car/toon _ __/_ __ _ ________ ________

pass/word _ _ __/_ __ _ ________ ________

arm/chair __ _/__ ___ ________ ________

laugh/ing _ __ __/_ __ ________ ________

calm/ly _ __ _/_ _ ________ ________

harm/ful _ __ _/_ _ _ ________ ________

farm/yard _ __ _/_ __ _ ________ ________

Two Syllable Words

This section is in three parts: Word Lists, Word Cards and Worksheets.

Word Lists

There is a list of two syllable words for each of the main vowel phonemes. They are in the order in which they are presented in the Extended Code of the Sounds~Write programme. These phonemes are found in Phases 3, 4 and 5 of Letters and Sounds.

The lists are comprised of words containing the target sound plus any other sounds previously taught.

Word Cards

There are pages of two syllable words which can be printed, laminated and cut up to use as word cards for word reading and writing.

These cards can also be used as word puzzles:

1. Print, laminate and cut the word list into separate words.
2. Cut each word into 2 syllables, as a puzzle. Make each one a different pattern, as illustrated below.
3. Put into packs of 8-10 words in small envelopes or cash bags.

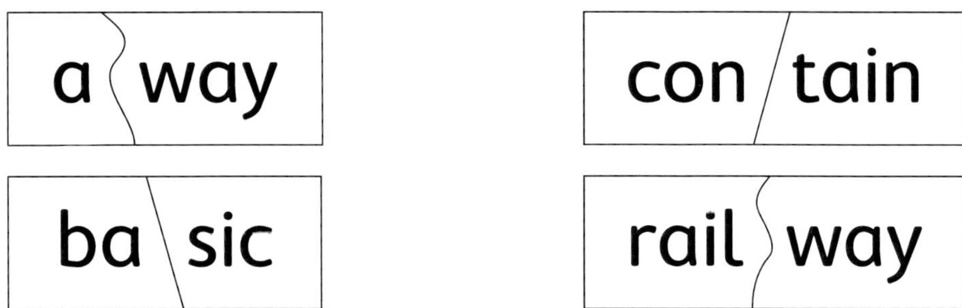

Using the Word Puzzles

4. Learners find all the first syllables by looking for the straight edge on the left, then say the first syllable. They complete each puzzle by finding the second syllable. Learners should say the syllables then the whole word.
5. When all the words are complete, write the words saying the sounds and the syllables, then the word.
6. More competent learners could then put each word into a sentence.

Worksheets

There are two pages for practising writing two syllable words. The words are presented in two syllables. Encourage the learners to read the word first: saying the sounds and the first syllable; then the sounds and the second syllable; then the whole word. They then write the word, saying the sounds and syllables as they write. There is a line underneath for the learners to write the word again without the gap.

There are also two worksheets presented as gap-fill exercises, where the learners choose a word from the box to complete the sentences.

'ae'

afraid
again
amaze
April
await
awake
away
baking
basic
blameless
braking
caveman
contain
crayfish
crayon
David
daybreak
display
enslave
handbrake
handstand
haystack
lampshade
makeup
mistake
nailbrush
nickname
painless
pancake
pavement
railway
sunbathe
Sunday
vacant
waitress

'ee'

agree
athlete
begin
believe
beneath
betray
between
briefcase
canteen
cheesecake
chimney
coffee
complete
concrete
crazy
creeping
daily
daydream
decrease
delay
delete
depend
depress
disease
eighteen
empty
equip
extreme
female
fifteen
filthy
freedom
freezing
frequent
freewheel
greeting
kidney
leapfrog
peanut
pretend
prevent
reading
reflect
regret
relax
release
repay
respect
result
reveal
safety
seasick
season
seaweed
secret
select
teaching
teapot
toffee
trapeze
twenty
ugly
windscreen

'oe'

alone
arrow
awoke
backbone
barrow
boatload
bolthole
borrow
broken
Congo
control
crossbow
crossroad
ditto
explode
fishbowl
goldfish
growbag
lamppost
maypole
nosebleed
peephole
postbox
postcode
pothole
protect
remote
roadblock
robot
scapegoat
shadow
shallow
snowflake
toecap
trombone
window
yellow
zero

'er'

alert
amber
anger
birthday
bitter
blackbird
blister
bowler
buffer
burglar
burning
busker
butter
camper
canter
cavern
chapter
cheddar
clockwork
cobbler
collar
conker
cracker
crater
creeper
crossword
custard
dagger
dealer
deserve
dinner
dirty
disturb
dollar
dreamer
duster
eager
early
earthquake
earthworm
Easter
effort
enter
expert
filter
finger
furnish
glitter
hammer
hamster
hermit
jumper
lobster
mirror
monster
never
number
perfect
perhaps
return
roadworks
rubber
silver
sister
splinter
sunburn
thunder
transfer

'e'

absent
address
against
arrest
attempt
attend
bedstead
blockhead
breakfast
breathless
cadet
cassette
checkup
cherry
cherub
chestnut
chicken
collect
comment
complex
connect
consent
content
contest
convex
correct
credit
crumpet
dentist
depend
depress
distress
dressing
edit
effect
eggshell
ending
enter
escape
event
exact
exempt
exist
exit
extinct
feather
frequent
friendship
headdress
headwind
headfirst
headlamp
helmet
helpless
invent
mattress
neglect
never
nutmeg
object
often
perfect
pregnant
present
pretend
protect
puppet
second
select
trumpet
yellow

'ow'

about

allow

aloud

around

cloudy

counting

county

cowshed

cutout

download

fountain

mountain

outing

surround

'oo' (as in moon)

baboon
bamboo
bathroom
bassoon
bedroom
beetroot
bluebell
bluebird
blueprint
booster
broomstick
canoe
classroom
exclude
fluid
foolish
fruitcake
gluing
guestroom
include
legroom
lupin
monsoon
moonbeam
moody
mushroom
playroom
shampoo
shoelace
soupspoon
suitcase
super
teaspoon
today
unscrew

'ie'

admire
alight
arrive
bagpipes
baptize
baseline
beehive
behind
blowpipe
brighter
brightness
capsize
childproof
China
Chinese
coastline
crisis
daylight
deadline
define
delight
describe
direct
dislike
driver
fighter
final
gunfire
handwrite
headlight
landslide
lighthouse
lightning
linesman
magpie
moonlight
nightcap
nightclub
nightgown
nineteen
outline
pipeline
playtime
prescribe
seaside
spaceflight
spider
survive
surprise
tonight
upright
writing

'oo' (as in book)

bookcase

bookshop

bookrest

bookworm

bulldog

bullfrog

cooker

crooked

fulfil

grateful

painful

pulling

pushing

textbook

thankful

woodwork

'or'

absorb
acorn
afford
almost
also
alter
although
August
autumn
award
ballroom
before
broadcast
corkscrew
corner
cornet
cornflake
dashboard
daughter
doorway
drawing
escort
export
fallen
forbid
forklift
forward
morning
paintball
passport
popcorn
porthole
portrait
report
reward
scoreboard
seashore
snowboard
spacewalk
support
sweetcorn
swordfish
towards
walking

'air'

aircrew

airline

airlock

airmail

airman

airport

airtight

bareback

barely

beachwear

bearskin

beware

careless

chairman

elsewhere

fairly

nightmare

nowhere

repair

scarecrow

software

staircase

therefore

wheelchair

whereas

'ar'

advance
after
alarm
archer
argue
armchair
armful
armpit
armrest
artist
bargain
barley
bathmat
bathroom
bathtub
birdbath
bizarre
bombard
carbon
cargo
carpet
carport
carton
cartoon
cartridge
cartwheel
charcoal
charming
classroom
enlarge
farmhouse
farmyard
fasten
father
gargoyle
halfway
harmful
harmless
harpoon
harvest
heartbeat
pardon
parking
parkland
parsnip
partner
passing
passport
password
postcard
pathway
scarlet
starfish
starling
target
tarnish
varnish

afraid	again
amaze	April
apron	await
awake	away
bacon	baking
basement	basic
blameless	braking
caveman	contain
David	daybreak
enslave	gangway

gateway	handbrake
handshake	haystack
lampshade	makeup
mistake	nailbrush
nickname	painless
pancake	pavement
playing	railway
raining	sailing
shaking	Sunday
vacant	waitress

agree	athlete
begin	believe
beneath	between
cheesecake	chimney
coffee	complete
crazy	daily
delay	delete
depend	eighteen
extreme	female
fifteen	frequent

kidney	pretend
prevent	reading
reason	relax
repay	respect
result	safety
seasick	secret
squeaky	teaching
teapot	toffee
trapeze	twenty
ugly	very

approach	arrow
awoke	backbone
boatload	bolthole
borrow	control
crossroad	enclose
explode	follow
glowing	joking
lamppost	lonely
maypole	mostly
mowing	peephole

postcode	postman
pothole	protect
remote	roadblock
roasting	robot
shollow	showcase
slowly	snowflake
snowing	spoken
toecap	total
towing	window
yellow	zero

alert	anger
birthday	blackbird
blister	burning
butter	camper
chapter	cheddar
collar	counter
deserve	dinner
dirty	duster
eager	early
effort	enter

expert	finger
flower	furnish
hammer	jumper
learning	lobster
never	return
silver	sister
thirty	thunder
tower	transfer
trousers	turnip
tweezers	waiter

against	arrest
bedstead	breakfast
breathless	connect
distress	eggshell
enter	feather
friendship	headdress
headlamp	helpless
never	perfect
pregnant	weather

about	allow
aloud	around
cloudy	counting
county	cowshed
download	fountain
growling	loudly
mountain	outing
shouted	shower
surround	tower

baboon	balloon
bamboo	bassoon
bathroom	bedroom
beetroot	bluebell
bluebird	booster
broomstick	canoe
chewing	classroom
coupon	doing
exclude	fluid
foolish	fruitcake

gluing	grooming
include	into
legroom	loophole
monsoon	moody
moving	mushroom
playroom	rooftop
ruin	shampoo
sooner	suitcase
super	teaspoon
today	truly

admire	arrive
behind	beside
brighter	childproof
China	coastline
collide	crisis
daylight	deadline
delight	describe
direct	dislike
fighter	final
fireman	flying

Friday	frostbite
headlight	July
landslide	lighthouse
lightning	magpie
myself	nightclub
nineteen	outline
prescribe	retire
seaside	spider
surprise	triumph
trying	writing

bookcase	bookshop
bulldog	bullfrog
cookbook	cooker
couldn't	crooked
fulfil	grateful
painful	pulling
pushing	shouldn't
textbook	thankful
woodwork	wouldn't

afford	almost
also	alter
although	always
August	author
autumn	award
before	blackboard
corkscrew	corner
cornflake	dashboard
doorway	daughter
drawing	export
fallen	floorboard
forget	forgive
forklift	forward

ignore	naughty
paintball	portrait
report	reward
scoreboard	seashore
slaughter	support
thoughtless	walking
wardrobe	yawning

airfield	airline
airmail	armchair
beachwear	beware
brassware	careful
careless	elsewhere
fairly	nowhere
repair	software
staircase	therefore
wearing	whereas

advance	after
alarm	artist
bargain	bathroom
birdbath	bookmark
calmly	carpet
carport	cartoon
cartwheel	charcoal
charming	classroom
dancing	enlarge
farmhouse	farmyard

fasten	father
glasses	halfway
harmful	harmless
harpoon	harvest
pardon	parsnip
partner	passing
passport	postcard
scarlet	starling
target	varnish

Two Syllable Words

Read the word. Write one syllable on each line and then the whole word underneath:

coff-ee	____ ____ ________	to-day	____ ____ ________
yell-ow	____ ____ ________	pepp-er	____ ____ ________
lo-rry	____ ____ ________	bed-room	____ ____ ________
Sun-day	____ ____ ________	num-ber	____ ____ ________
happ-y	____ ____ ________	win-dow	____ ____ ________
birth-day	____ ____ ________	tea-pot	____ ____ ________
eigh-teen	____ ____ ________	flow-er	____ ____ ________
sis-ter	____ ____ ________	sham-poo	____ ____ ________
A-pril	____ ____ ________	toast-er	____ ____ ________

Two Syllable Words

Read the word. Write one syllable on each line and then the whole word underneath:

jump-er	_____ _____ __________	cu-rry	_____ _____ __________
train-ers	_____ _____ __________	pain-ful	_____ _____ __________
eight-y	_____ _____ __________	sunn-y	_____ _____ __________
sil-ver	_____ _____ __________	butt-er	_____ _____ __________
six-ty	_____ _____ __________	Fri-day	_____ _____ __________
lo-rry	_____ _____ __________	fif-teen	_____ _____ __________
doc-tor	_____ _____ __________	Thurs-day	_____ _____ __________
thun-der	_____ _____ __________	bath-room	_____ _____ __________
bur-ger	_____ _____ __________	cloud-y	_____ _____ __________

Choose a word from the box for each sentence:

carpet	summer	reading	bedroom	driver
sister	tonight	window	fifteen	coffee

1. We will go camping next ________.
2. I can meet you for ________ at ten thirty.
3. Shall we watch a film ________?
4. I am ________ a good book.
5. The drink got spilt on the ________.
6. The ________ was left open.
7. We will paint the ________ at the weekend.
8. My ________ is older than me.
9. Jack was ________ in May.
10. He wants to be a taxi ________.

Choose a word from the box for each sentence:

forty	seaside	yellow	letter	finger
slowly	window	today	spider	shower

1. I must post this ________.

2. Steve cut his ________ on the glass.

3. It may rain ________.

4. We go to the ________ every July.

5. Dave drives ________ up the road.

6. I look out of the ________.

7. The bird is black and ________.

8. I have a ________ every morning.

9. The ________ spins a web.

10. Karim will be ________ on his birthday.

Suffixes

Suffixes can be decoded but it is useful for learners to be able to recognise them before they get to that advanced level. It will enable them to read and spell many longer words and help to boost their self-esteem. It is therefore useful to teach the suffixes as whole units or syllables.

There are pages for reading and spelling the most common spellings of the most common suffixes:

'shun' - <tion>, <cian>

'zhun' - <sion>, <ssion>

'cher' - <ture>

'shul' - <tial>, <cial>

'shus' - <cious>, <tious>

The words are presented in syllables. The learners should read each syllable and then the word. They then write the word, saying the sounds and syllables as they go; firstly in separate syllables and then as a whole word.

Suffix – 'shun'

Read the word. Write one syllable on each line and then the whole word:

ac – tion ___ ___ ______

sta-tion ___ ___ ______

men – tion ___ ___ ______

lo – ca – tion ___ ___ ___ ______

ma – gi – cian ___ ___ ___ ______

a – tten – tion ___ ___ ___ ______

op - ti – cian ___ ___ ___ ______

di – rec – tion ___ ___ ___ ______

in – spec – tion ___ ___ ___ ______

e – lec – tri – cian _ ___ ___ ___ ______

med – i – ca – tion ___ _ ___ ___ ______

pol – i – ti – cian ___ _ ___ ___ ______

op – er – a – tion ___ ___ _ ___ ______

Suffix – 'zhun'

Read the word. Write one syllable on each line and then the whole word:

vi – sion ____ ____ ________

di – vi – sion ____ ____ ____ ________

re – vi – sion ____ ____ ____ ________

con – fe – ssion ____ ____ ____ ________

in – va – sion ____ ____ ____ ________

o - cca – sion ____ ____ ____ ________

con – fu – sion ____ ____ ____ ________

ex – plo – sion ____ ____ ____ ________

di – ver – sion ____ ____ ____ ________

coll – i – sion ____ ____ ____ ________

trans – fu – sion ____ ____ ____ ________

tel-e-vi-sion ____ ____ ____ ____ ________

su – per – vi – sion ____ ____ ____ ____ ________

po – sse – ssion ____ ____ ____ ________

Suffix – 'cher'

Read the word. Write one syllable on each line and then the whole word:

mix – ture ____ ____ ____________

pic – ture ____ ____ ____________

tex – ture ____ ____ ____________

mois – ture ____ ____ ____________

punc – ture ____ ____ ____________

crea – ture ____ ____ ____________

struc – ture ____ ____ ____________

ad – ven – ture ____ ____ ____ ____________

fur - ni – ture ____ ____ ____ ____________

Suffix – 'zher'

plea – sure ____ ____ ____________

trea – sure ____ ____ ____________

mea – sure ____ ____ ____________

Suffix – 'shul'

Read the word. Write one syllable on each line and then the whole word:

so – cial ____ ____ __________

spe – cial ____ ____ __________

in – i – tial ____ ____ ____ __________

off – i – cial ____ ____ ____ __________

e – ssen – tial ____ ____ ____ __________

po – ten – tial ____ ____ ____ __________

sub – stan – tial ____ ____ ____ __________

to – rren – tial ____ ____ ____ __________

ar – ti – fi – cial ____ ____ ____ ____ __________

con – fi – den – cial ____ ____ ____ ____ __________

Suffix – 'shus'

Read the word. Write one syllable on each line and then the whole word:

vi – cious ______ ______ ______________

pre – cious ______ ______ ______________

cau – tious ______ ______ ______________

con – scious ______ ______ ______________

nu – tri - tious ______ ______ ______ ______________

de – li – cious ______ ______ ______ ______________

ma - li – cious ______ ______ ______ ______________

a – tro – cious ______ ______ ______ ______________

pre – co – cious ______ ______ ______ ______________

fic – ti – cious ______ ______ ______ ______________

Suffix – 'kshus'

an – xious ______ ______ ______________

ob – no – xious ______ ______ ______ ______________